Reliable School Leadership

Reliable School Leadership

What All Students Deserve

Jeff Swensson and Lynn Lehman

ROWMAN & LITTLEFIELD
Lanham • Boulder • New York • London

Published by Rowman & Littlefield
An imprint of The Rowman & Littlefield Publishing Group, Inc.
4501 Forbes Boulevard, Suite 200, Lanham, Maryland 20706
www.rowman.com

6 Tinworth Street, London SE11 5AL, United Kingdom

Copyright © 2021 by Jeff Swensson and Lynn Lehman

All rights reserved. No part of this book may be reproduced in any form or by any electronic or mechanical means, including information storage and retrieval systems, without written permission from the publisher, except by a reviewer who may quote passages in a review.

British Library Cataloguing in Publication Information Available

Library of Congress Cataloging-in-Publication Data

Names: Swensson, Jeff, author. | Lehman, Lynn E. (Lynn Edward), 1947- author.
Title: Reliable school leadership : what all students deserve / Jeff Swensson and Lynn Lehman.
Description: Lanham, Maryland : Rowman & Littlefield, 2021. | Includes bibliographical references and index. | Summary: "This book reimagines educational leadership on behalf of all students. Functional educational leadership-action and agency for reliability-is the theme shared with educators. To thwart the disconnections caused by standardized accountability, function of educational leadership is offered as a tool to construct reliable teaching and learning"—Provided by publisher.
Identifiers: LCCN 2020054915 (print) | LCCN 2020054916 (ebook) | ISBN 9781475859713 (cloth) | ISBN 9781475859720 (paperback) | ISBN 9781475859737 (epub)
Subjects: LCSH: Educational leadership—United States. | School management and organization—United States.
Classification: LCC LB2805 .S86 2021 (print) | LCC LB2805 (ebook) | DDC 371.2—dc23
LC record available at https://lccn.loc.gov/2020054915
LC ebook record available at https://lccn.loc.gov/2020054916

Contents

Preface   xi

Introduction   1

1   The Issue with Educational Leadership   3
    What Is Leadership, Anyway?   4
        From the Factory Floor to the Classroom: Educational Leadership   4
        Where Does Educational Leadership Begin?   5
        So, What Does a School Leader Sign Up For?   5
    Virtue and Educational Leadership   6
        Virtue: An All-Encompassing Excellence   7
        Virtue and the Worth of Leadership   7
    Crucial Relationships and Leadership   8
        Relationships: First among Equals   8
        Relationships: Over-Choice   9
        Relationships: Disconnected   9
        Relationships: Imposed   10
        Relationships: Limited   10
    What's a School Leader to Do?   10
    Is Leadership a Pattern-Seeking Device?   12
        Theories and Styles and Patterns, Oh My!   12
    What Should Leaders Know to Serve All Students?   13
    Looking at This Chapter in the Rearview Mirror   13

2   It's NOT All About You   15
    An Intervening Note   16
    The Troubled History of Educational Leadership   17
        Organizational Leadership First and Foremost   17
        Virtue-Free Leadership   18

	Mirror, Mirror, on My Wall: A Leadership Syndrome	19
	The Origins of Educational Leadership	20
	The Commitments of an Educational Leader	20
	Commitment #1: Moral Obligation of Public Education	21
	Commitment #2: Poly-Collegial Leadership	22
	The Conjunction of Leadership Commitments: *Leading-Out*	22
	The Greater Good and Educational Leadership	23
	A Coda to This Cautionary Tale	23
	Looking at This Chapter in the Rearview Mirror	26
3	I Don't Think I've Ever Seen So Many Trees	29
	Educational Leadership: Tree Identification	30
	The Pitfalls of Educational Leadership	31
	Old Growth, Second Growth, and the Weeds	32
	Old Growth Educational Leadership	32
	Second Growth Educational Leadership	33
	Educational Leadership Down in the Weeds	35
	Management as Product	35
	Educational Leadership Is Stuck	36
	Is There a Forest among Those Trees?	38
	The Forest: Functional Educational Leadership	39
	Educational Leadership in the Indeterminate Zone	39
	Looking at This Chapter in the Rearview Mirror	41
4	Wheat and Chaff: Educational Leadership Uncovered	43
	The Advent of Function of Leadership	43
	Educational Leadership as an Ecological System	44
	The Double Helix and Functional Educational Leadership	45
	A Return to Ninth-Grade Biology	46
	The Theory and Utility of the Double Helix	46
	Toward Functional Educational Leadership: A Definition	47
	The Double Helix: Shaping Educational Leadership	47
	Harvesting Educational Leadership	48
	Can Educational Leadership Function Reliably?	48
	Looking at This Chapter in the Rearview Mirror	50
5	Our Students Deserve—Dynamic Instruction	53
	The Case for Dynamic Instruction as Function	54
	Why Leadership and Instruction Disconnect	54
	Leadership *of Instruction* and Leadership *for Instruction*	55
	Leadership *of Instruction*	55
	Leadership *for Instruction*	56
	The Original Power of Education	57

	If Instructional Leadership Fell in a Classroom, Would It Make a Sound?	58
	The Interminable Cacophony of Standardized Testing	59
	Marooned on the Island of Default Culture	60
	Transforming Backward in the Default Culture	60
	Functional Educational Leadership: Agency and Action	61
	Action for Functional Educational Leadership	61
	Dynamic Instruction in a Leader's Day	62
	The Pedagogies of Dynamic Instruction	63
	Can Educational Leadership Pivot?	64
	Pivot Opportunity #1	64
	Pivot Opportunity #2	65
	Pivot Opportunity #3	65
	Dynamic Instruction: A Rung That Students Deserve	66
	Looking at This Chapter in the Rearview Mirror	67
6	Our Students Deserve—Ethical Leadership	69
	The Rationale for Ethics in Leadership	69
	Using Ethics Is Not the Same as *Being* Ethical	70
	Present-Day Upside Down Ethics	72
	Singularity and the Hard Work of *Being* Ethical	73
	Is There a "How" of *Being* Ethical?	74
	Integrity and *Being* Ethical	75
	A Different Leadership Responsibility	76
	Reflection as Ethical Agency	76
	Choosing Ethics Intentionally	77
	Direct Effects and Ethical Leadership	78
	Direct Effects of *Being* Ethical	78
	Looking at This Chapter in the Rearview Mirror	79
7	Our Students Deserve—Emotionally Intelligent Leadership	81
	Wherefore Art Thou, Emotional Intelligence (EI)?	81
	Intelligence and Leadership: A Blast from the Past	82
	Leaders and an Incomplete Map	82
	The Behaviors of Emotional Intelligence (EI)	83
	Social Skills: The Pea Under the Leadership Mattress	84
	How Annoying! Emotions Interrupt Rationality	84
	Emotional Intelligence (EI): A Set of Abilities	85
	The Ability Model of Emotional Intelligence (EI)	85
	Emotional Intelligence (EI) in a Leader's Day	86
	Emotional Intelligence (EI) and the Limbic System	87
	Emotional Intelligence (EI) and Academic Performance	87
	Emotional Intelligence (EI) and Dynamic Instruction	88

	Emotional Intelligence (EI) and Its Influence on Colleagues	89
	The Value of Emotional Intelligence (EI)	89
	Leadership and the Emotionally Intelligent School	90
	Looking at This Chapter in the Rearview Mirror	92
8	**Our Students Deserve—Public Life Education**	**93**
	The Erosion of Citizenship Education	95
	Public Life and Mutuality	95
	School Leadership and Public Life	96
	Public Education: A Habit of Public Creation	96
	A Funny Thing Happened on the Way to Citizenship Education	97
	Islanding: Land's End for the Intelligence of Social Balance	97
	If Everyone Is an Island	98
	The Premise of *Islanding*	98
	Public Life Education: A Transformational Leadership Function	100
	Enacting a Transformation	100
	Public Life Education and Democracy	101
	Public Life Education and Dissent	102
	The Public Thing We're Looking For	104
	Looking at This Chapter in the Rearview Mirror	105
9	**Enacting Functional School Leadership**	**107**
	A Return to the Indeterminate Zone of Educational Leadership	108
	Marbles Throughout the Indeterminate Zone	108
	Echo Leadership	110
	Finding the Voice of Function of Leadership	111
	Picturing Functional Educational Leadership	111
	In the Picture: The Systemic Ecology of Intentionality	111
	Function and the Construction of Educational Leadership	113
	Functional Educational Leadership Is Public Work	113
	How to Function as an Educational Leader	114
	Misperceptions of Function and Educational Leadership	115
	Looking at This Chapter in the Rearview Mirror	116
10	**Details, Details, Details**	**117**
	Details Send Signals and Signals Are Messages	117
	Leadership of Details: Anticipation and Assessment	118
	Trust Is a Detail	119
	Detail-Oriented Leadership	119
	Inquiring for "Returns"	120
	Surveying for "Returns"	120
	Gardening for "Returns"	122
	Indignity Can Be in the Details	123

	Attention to Detail: A Leader's Message	124
	So Many Detail-Oriented Observers	125
	Looking at This Chapter in the Rearview Mirror	125
11	Reliable Educational Leadership	127
	The Ecology of Reliable Educational Leadership	128
	What *Should Be* the Expectations for US Public Education?	128
	The Expectation of Virtue	129
	From Virtue: The Expectation of Reliability	129
	Reliability and the Ecology of Educational Environments	130
	Ecological Principles for Reliable Leadership	131
	The "Voice" of Reliability	132
	The Active Person and Reliable Leadership	133
	Speaking to Highly Reliable Educational Leadership	133
	What *Are* the Expectations for US Public Education?	134
	What Are the Expectations of Function?	136
	Looking at This Chapter in the Rearview Mirror	136
12	So Much Leadership, So Little Time	139
	Educational Leadership: Nothing Less Than the Future	140
	Looking for Panaceas in Pandora's Box	140
	Expectations, Function, and the Future of Educational Leadership	141
	Function: The Ecology of Leadership and the Ecology of Thought	143
	Function as Competency	143
	Functional Educational Leadership and *the Good* and Democracy	145
	Educational Leaders as Moral Agents	146
	Agentic Educational Leadership	146
	The Inescapable Dilemma of Leadership	148
	Agency for Functional Educational Leadership	148
	Educational Expectations Are the Future of Agency	149
	Functional Educational Leadership: Working the Work	150
	Speaking of Functional Educational Leadership	151
	Looking at This Book through the Windshield	152

References 155

Index 165

About the Authors 169

Preface

On the one hand, educational leadership is beset by conceptual wrangling, disparate perspectives, and unfocused practice. As a result, educational leadership is the equivalent of an unmatched sock. Scholarly confusion and practical uncertainties confront school leaders with a mishmash of unrelated theories, styles, models, and innovations. Educational leaders struggle with unrelated research, disconnected ideologies, and counterproductive mandates as if these can be matched reliably.

On the other hand, educational leadership earns kudos for its positive impact on a host of significant school attributes and outcomes including student achievement, school climate, teacher morale, and community engagement. School and school district progress, student success, and continuous improvement are influenced when leaders function effectively.

Present-day educational leadership is called to meet a wide range of disparate expectations. The practice of school leadership, as a result, is replete with anomalies; *reliable leadership* is more of an oxymoron than a reality.

Prevailing attempts to establish reliable school leadership are often tied to terms like *management* or *administration* whose pedigree lies in rational thinking, hierarchies, bureaucracy, and/or free market theory. These notions are aligned with societal and ideological factors that envision a businesslike approach to teaching and learning that school leaders should adopt universally.

Caught amidst these conflicting expressions, America's students metaphorically await a resolution. Are school leaders merely managers and should school management replicate the efficiency alleged to create successful business leadership? Or, is it possible to function as a school leader on behalf of all students, avoid the pitfalls of America's educational history, and reimagine educational leadership?

The answers to these questions depend on the choices made by educational leaders and the intentions that underlie the choices and the professional practices that ensue. Above all, the answers to questions about the purpose and impact of educational leadership during the remainder of the twenty-first century depend on whether school leaders can enact their own professional transformation.

Educational leadership for the remainder of the twenty-first century will face challenges that status quo notions of leading do not resolve successfully. Establishing the future educational environments that all US public school students deserve demands an intentionality and focus that present-day leadership training, staff development, and practice do not deliver. School leaders during the next eight decades need capacities that build on and surpass the leadership status quo.

The purpose of this book is to immerse educational leaders, prospective leaders, and all US public educators in a dialogue that identifies and explores the functions necessary to reimagine school leadership. Educational leadership must transform itself if it is to grow its potential and inspire students and professional colleagues.

The authors of this book have no illusions about the challenges that face public educators in present-day America. We have served in a variety of roles and contexts—teacher, team leader, assistant principal, principal, assistant superintendent, and superintendent; in urban, suburban, and rural schools—and learned from our colleagues, community members, and students. We have seen the damage done by the age of accountability and by ideologies that disdain the professionalism and care that suffuse public school classrooms throughout the United States.

In recognition of the battle being fought to fulfill the promises of public education for all students, this book sheds light on the ideas and practices that leadership can embrace to deliver these promises reliably. The value of educational leadership cannot be ignored but this value is forsaken if we do not choose to enact functional educational leadership in our day-to-day practice.

Jeff Swensson
Lynn Lehman
Spring 2021

Introduction

This book is organized to support, inform, challenge, and inspire leaders, prospective leaders, and colleagues throughout US public education. Because school leadership cannot be a recipe, because leadership demands keeping an "eye on the prize," and because leadership is a dense combination of opportunities, challenges, and choices, this book is organized to reimagine educational leadership.

To transform how educational leadership fulfills its obligations to all students, it's necessary to understand present-day leadership and the issues that disconnect it from reliability and function. To this end, the first two chapters examine how leadership generally, and educational leadership specifically, are shaped by research and practice. The misguided outcomes and choices that emerge when the nature of educational leadership is unclear or when individual leaders make choices that benefit only themselves are discussed.

From this beginning, an overview of the vast array of theories, styles, and models of educational leadership is shared in chapter 3. The multitude of concepts about educational leadership ensures that educational leaders cannot see the forest for the trees. A more effective, comprehensive, understanding of and approach to school leadership develops when the kernel of educational leadership is identified in chapter 4.

Reimagining educational leadership and transforming what US students deserve from public education during the remainder of the twenty-first century is explored in chapters 5, 6, 7, and 8. Four functions—one in each of these chapters—are explained.

These four functions—dynamic instruction, ethical leadership, emotional intelligence, and public life education—represent the intentionality and self-efficacy required if twenty-first century school leaders are to foster reliable educational leadership. The enactment of *functional educational leadership* is discussed in chapter 9. Chapter 10 explores the messages within details that leadership must anticipate and assess to maximize the positive effects of functions of leadership.

Chapters 11 and 12 argue for reimagining educational leadership in relationship to function. These chapters describe the leadership necessary and sufficient to make a difference for all students in US public schools. Functional educational leadership is proposed as the educator-initiated transformation that brings reliability to school leadership.

Chapter 1

The Issue with Educational Leadership

"If you don't know where you're going, you probably won't know when you get there."

—Yogi Berra in Hallinger and Heck, 2002, p. 18

At first glance, the extensive scholarly and practical attention paid to educational leadership seems more than sufficient to render it well-understood and reliable. It appears that educational leadership knows where it's going. The issue with educational leadership, however, is that the opposite is true. Paradoxically, the scope and breadth of scholarly and practical attention devoted to leadership in US public schools contributes significantly to uncertainty, disconnection, and unreliability.

What lies ahead in this chapter is a bird's-eye view of both leadership in general and public school leadership, in particular. The purpose of this discussion is to engage readers with questions that demand answers if educational leadership is to engage all students with the teaching and learning that they deserve.

Educators, policymakers, school stakeholders, and political leaders who encounter the ideas in this chapter should prepare to reflect on their own sense of school leadership and whether this view embraces reliable educational leadership. This chapter encourages reflection via these questions:

- What is leadership?
- Where does educational leadership "begin"?
- What are the professional relationships of educational leadership?
- What does a school leader do?
- Can leadership be a pattern-seeking device?
- What should leaders know to serve all students?

WHAT IS LEADERSHIP, ANYWAY?

Leith, as Senge, Hamilton and Kania (2015) tell us, is the Indo-European root of *to lead*. This root word "literally means to step across a threshold—and to let go of whatever might limit stepping forward" (Senge, Hamilton, and Kania, 2015, p. 2).

Early scholarly investigation of leadership is focused on individual efficiency in business and industry. This research stepped across a threshold in the sense that it created a new academic discipline and a definition for leadership as "the process of influencing the activities of an organized group toward goal setting and goal accomplishment" (Beare, Caldwell, and Millikan, 1989, p. 101).

Early findings about leadership in business and industry forged an enduring perspective about the nature of leading. Scholarship and practice galvanized America's understanding of leadership to "individuals who inhabit formal positions of power, and possess traits such as assertiveness, decisiveness, control, and domination (Fletcher, 2004)" (Douglass, 2018, p. 388). Eagly and Chen (2010) note that "people generally believe that leaders are ambitious, confident, self-sufficient, and dominant, that is, well endowed with agentic and competent qualities (Powell, Butterfield, and Parent, 2002; Schein, 2001)" (p. 217).

From the Factory Floor to the Classroom: Educational Leadership

Gravitating to studies about efficient business leadership, early educational scholars and practitioners guaranteed that educational leadership would be "a profession anchored in the sub-domains of business" (Murphy, Neumerski, Goldring, Grissom, and Porter, 2016, p. 463).

Educational researchers echoed leadership insights from the business world including that "the personal qualities of school administrators have a big impact on what they do, how they do it, and how well they do it" (Greenfield, 2004, p. 190). These studies called attention to *charismatic leadership*—also referenced as *great man leadership theory*—and gave credence to natural-born characteristics as a centerpiece of efficient management in successful schools.

When educators adopted theories and styles of leadership from business, they responded to "guidance for the emergence of a post-teaching-based profession. School leaders were now corporate managers, adherents of the principles of management (Callahan, 1962; Tyack and Hansot, 1982)" (Murphy et al., 2016, p. 463).

Early research about efficient management also identified *scientific management* and *classical bureaucratic theory* (see textbox 2.1). These concepts were "borrowed from the business world [and] co-opted to facilitate the implementation of the many imperatives and projects required of educational administrators" (Rice, 2017, p. 55). A thriving cottage industry emerged and ground out a myriad theories and styles about educational leadership. These theories, styles, and models rolled from the factory floor into US schools to establish inconsistencies and disconnections throughout research for and practice of educational leadership (Beare, Caldwell, and Millikan, 1989; Latta, 2019; Yukl, 2012).

Where Does Educational Leadership Begin?

Educational leadership springs from scholarship and research about efficient leadership in business organizations. As a result, educational leadership begins with fundamental concerns about reliability: the degree to which specifications about educational leadership can be depended upon to be accurate and function to fulfill the promises and expectations of US public education is open to question. Scholars and practitioners struggle to enact educational leadership that yields more than management, efficiency, and bureaucracy.

Some scholars suggest elements of leadership that, if untangled from the morass of management, identify the metaphoric first steps that school leaders must take to jettison business leadership and move forward to reliable school leadership. Yukl's (2012) observation that "the essence of leadership in organizations is influencing and facilitating individual and collective efforts to accomplish shared objectives" (p. 66) suggests one of these first steps. But a paradigm shift is required if this simple observation is to grow the scholarship for and practice of educational leadership in US public schools that all students deserve.

The complexity of this shift is illuminated by Ciulla, Knights, Maybe, and Tompkins (2018) who note that educational leadership is "a complex moral relationship between people, based on trust, obligation, emotion, and some shared vision of the good" (p. 2). Van Wart (2013) adds that "leadership itself is constantly being socially constructed, making it both subjective and a moving target" (p. 562).

So, What Does a School Leader Sign Up For?

Public educators sign up for "the uncertainty, turbulence, messiness, and unpredictability of the milieu of schooling" (Goldring and Greenfield, 2002, p. 2). School leaders sign up for jobs within this milieu that are important, confusing, contradictory, gratifying, exhausting, and transformative. The difficult importance of educational leadership implies that when school leaders sign up, they should do so realizing the wisdom in the time-honored lyric, "you knew the job was dangerous when you took it" ("Super Chicken" Cartoon Theme, YouTube).

Educational leaders sign up for responsibilities, obligations, and duties that depend on ethics, competencies, and the extent of each leader's commitment to:

- *Agency.* School leaders sign up for agency:

  Having agency is to attribute choice, decision, practice, and responsibility to a person's, an individual's, or a group's judgment outside natural and external causes, iron logic, laws of nature, and necessities. This is why agency is referred to as "free will," "knowing right and wrong," "soul," "fault," "sin," "authorship," "praise," "addressee," "respondent," and so on. (Matusov, von Duyke, and Kayumova, 2016, p. 422)

- *Dedication.* Dedication to agency on behalf of students is a school leader's pursuit of reliability. Dedication at the building level, for example, is leadership's expression of professional practice sufficient and necessary to surmount four barriers: (1) the sheer number of roles that principals must fulfill, (2) the pace and infinite demands of an average workday that erode opportunities for instructional leadership, (3) few rewards for a school leader's focus on quality instruction, and (4) lack of knowledge about and lack of focus on the critical nature of student learning and how best to foster it (Murphy et al., 2016, pp. 463–464).
- *Obligation.* The moral obligation of public education and the values of this ethical commitment lie at the foundation of school leadership. But multiple conflicting demands assail educational leaders—including theories or mandates that espouse designated decisions, choices, or perspectives as *the* pathway to ethical leadership—and ensure that the obligation to take responsibility for ethics cannot be purely ethical, that is ethical from all points of view, all the time. "Thus, the predicament for leadership is that ethics is both necessary and impossible" (Ciulla et al., 2018, p. 10; Rhodes and Badham, 2018). Educational leadership's greatest obligation is to discover how to function reliably given substantial conundrums such as this.

VIRTUE AND EDUCATIONAL LEADERSHIP

Innumerable paradoxes confront, challenge, flummox, or inspire educators in their varied assignments. Educators fulfill their assigned role by meeting expectations and requirements embedded in policy, directives, mandates, curriculum, professional standards, statute, and, ultimately, the points of view of countless colleagues, students, parents/caregivers, and citizens.

Herein lies the origin of a question that practitioners and scholars must answer about the nature of educational leadership: Can school leadership reliably fulfill the expectation that leaders serve something greater than themselves?

To inquire about the reliability of educational leadership, educators are obligated to understand the expectations associated with public education and its leadership. Moreover, to inquire about educational leadership and reliability entails an obligation to understand the relationships that leaders must cultivate. Foremost among these is the relationship between educational leadership and *virtue*.

Virtue: An All-Encompassing Excellence

Obligations, responsibilities, and expectations that reliable leadership ought to fulfill are dependent upon the relationship between educational leadership and "virtue or *arête* [which] is an excellence that encompasses both ethics and competency" (Ciulla et al., 2018, p. 5).

Ethics and competency are foundational to all relationships involved in a leader's role. Without virtue, leadership in US public education exists in name only. Virtue constitutes the shared vision of *the good* necessary and sufficient to the competencies or functions of reliable educational leadership. Moreover, choices, decisions, and behaviors rooted in virtue, *the good*, permit a comprehensive transformation of the present-day understanding of educational adequacy (Swensson and Shaffer, 2020).

The imperative of virtue is the imperative for educational leaders to engage colleagues, students, and the school community with agency capable of stepping over the threshold of practices that otherwise limit a school or school district from moving forward into function.

Virtue and the Worth of Leadership

A relationship with virtue allows leaders to keep their fingers on the pulse of the worth of their leadership. Several outcomes demonstrate the necessity of this personal oversight. First, it is of the utmost importance that leaders judge their behaviors based on the fact that they are part of something bigger than themselves (Ciulla et al., 2018, p. 4).

Next, public school leadership entails an understanding of the responsibilities involved in public service in a democracy. Educational leadership, then, entails "building a sense of the 'we,' trusting others in shared forms of leadership and knowledge-building, empowering others as publics build capacity to make change, and transcending individualistic frames of knowledge and action (Knight Abowitz, 2014)" (Knight Abowitz, 2018, p. 11).

The third principle is an example of how educational leaders truly are part of something bigger than themselves. School leadership plays a significant role in the future of shared governance at the core of US democracy. "Shared governance is the assumption that citizens in democratic societies have a legitimate stake in the running of their society and should be educated to participate in that work" (Knight Abowitz and Stitzlein, 2018, p. 36). The relationship between public education, educational leadership, and the principles of US democracy is at center stage among the responsibilities of school leaders that speaks to the need for reliable public education.

CRUCIAL RELATIONSHIPS AND LEADERSHIP

Relationships at the core of educational leadership create, sustain, and improve educational environments that all students deserve. While these relationships deserve study and while this narrative will engage with the functions of educational leadership, establishing a sequence from "most important" to "least important" relationships is not a fruitful enterprise and will not be attempted here.

Relationships: First among Equals

Understanding that there is a relationship that is first among equals, however, is an essential development for the future of reliable educational leadership. The interdependence between competency and ethics, virtue in educational leadership, is expressed in the observation by Ciulla et al. (2018) that ethics are "deeply rooted in responsibility involving imagination and ability to see other viewpoints; willingness to judge for oneself; and willingness to act, and to pay for these actions, if need be" (p. 9). Competency and ethics merge to establish the relationship between educational leadership and the greater good.

This relationship is first among equals of the many professional relationships that educational leaders are called to enact within day-to-day practice. This relationship puts school leaders in position to avoid the false assumption that "schools exist as something disconnected from society" (Fraise and Brooks, 2015, p. 7). No practicing public educator would make this egregious error; society is omnipresent in school.

Leading, therefore, means engaging with a greater good to enhance all that society gives to, and to ameliorate all that society takes away from, students. The nature of educational leadership for the remainder of the twenty-first century and the nature of its impact on all students depends on the relationship of educational leadership with virtue.

Relationships: Over-Choice

Too many choices about the nature of educational leadership—styles, theories, practices, and so on—limit the capacity of educators to express virtue and to interconnect virtue with professional relationships. Over-choice about the nature of leadership in US schools overwhelms the capacity of leaders to function reliably.

So many visions—the mandates of policy, the claims of ideologues, the interventions of scholars, the protestations of politicians—call for so many iterations of leadership that school leaders cannot establish virtue reliably to foster the relationships critical to effective teaching and learning. "The leadership literature is plagued by weak, inconsistent, and contradictory findings" (Fernandez, 2005, p. 197).

Swimming upstream against a torrent of over-choice, educational leaders fail to heed the insight that success "is a function of 'the disciplined pursuit of less'" (Schmoker, 2019, p. 26). Over-choice obscures the justifiable presumption that a future, salient, relationship between school leadership and reliability depends on the simple idea "that successful schools have an orientation that focuses staff attention on improving student learning" (Hallinger and Heck, 2002, p. 16).

When ethics and competencies are hidden beneath over-choice and its frenzy for affixing labels to leading, the nature and practice of educational leadership can evade, ignore, or fall short of virtue.

Relationships: Disconnected

How educational leadership is understood in the present day is as much a collection of disconnected links as it is a chain. Conflicting perspectives and findings among and between multiple research findings, innumerable theories, and various definitions of educational leadership foster disconnections.

Urick and Bowers (2014) indicate, for example, that "unlike transformational leaders, instructional leaders do not work to build a climate" (p. 101). Bossert, Dwyer, Rowan, and Lee (1982), on the other hand, find that a principal's instructional leadership affects school climate and instructional organization and that both are linked to student achievement. Cohen, McCabe, Michelli, and Pickeral (2009) postulate, to the contrary, that school climate "is a group phenomenon that is larger than any one person's experience" (p. 180).

Disconnections across scholarship and between theory, statutes, and mandates prompt a broken chain of daily practices and ensure that educators often pick up random pieces of research, practice, intuition, or advice and glue them together as if this overlap constitutes leadership.

Relationships: Imposed

Educational leadership cannot escape relationships with external imperatives. Statutes, policies, political mandates—all impose what will be referred to as *ghost leadership*. Leadership ghosted upon school leaders by sources outside of education haunts day-to-day practice. Mandates, requirements, rules, statutes, and policies invented by politicians, policymakers, legislators, and others impose relationships on school leaders that undercut virtue and obviate reliability.

Some external imperatives impose relationships upon educational leaders that are nothing less than counterproductive. Free market schooling imperatives, for instance, "operate under a set of assumptions built on the economic definition of a public good that views education as only an individual experience sought to fulfill one's unique desires" (Knight Abowitz and Stitzlein, 2018, p. 34). The relationship between educational leadership and virtue in pursuit of the moral obligation of public education and the principles of US democracy, thus, is turned upside down.

Relationships: Limited

Over-choice, external imperatives, and disconnected links accumulate even when research focuses on students and the leaders they deserve (Theoharis, 2009). In addition, educational leadership encounters the myriad of societal influences daily. Social media, lived experience, religion, racism, language, bigotry, culture, economic downturns—all and more influence teaching, learning, and leadership. Amidst these influences, "principals are expected to be all things to all people and there is often little consensus on which activities should receive priority" (Murphy et al., 2016, p. 464).

The scholarly and practical response to this situation is a temptation to limit or restrict leadership competencies to the implementation of select theories and/or outcomes. One scholarly example of this phenomenon analyzes the perspectives of a small number of principals as the backdrop for "a specific discussion of social justice leadership (SJL)" (Theoharis, 2009, p. 1).

Although the value of social justice is well-documented (Santamaria, 2013), riveting leadership to any limitation, including this one, consigns educational leadership to preferred responses and relationships with little regard for context or reliability.

WHAT'S A SCHOOL LEADER TO DO?

Leaders do things. The anachronism of a principal anchored to his or her desk is just that, an out-of-date image. Anyone who has observed a school leader at work sees a whirlwind of activity. Sometimes, what a school leader does aligns well with virtue to foster excellence in the educational environment.

At other times, school leaders are sidetracked. Educational leaders too frequently engage competencies or pursue relationships that are investments in unreliability:

- *Change for its own sake:* Leadership and change often overlap. Leaders can and do make changes. But too often leaders are expected to change everything all the time. The damage done when leadership becomes a frenzy for change will be explored later in this discussion.
- *Reform as a mask:* Reform of US public education has become a cliché. Leaders are expected to promote reform with little attention paid to why. Reform is the mask that hides how policy, statute, and ideology obstruct reliable leadership.
- *A retrograde playbook:* Educators are stuck fulfilling a purpose that takes teaching, learning, and leadership backward. The purpose that drags public education away from satisfactory quality is the assumption that job placement is the primary reason why schools exist (Swensson and Shaffer, 2020).

In thrall to these inadequacies, some school leaders resort to prioritizing professional relationships with the randomness inherent in a game of whack-a-mole. Various iterations of leadership and the relationships created by leadership pop up—"constructivist, transformational, facilitative, instructional, developmental, distributed, or moral, for example" (Goldring and Greenfield, 2002, p. 1)—and leadership becomes a matter of hit or miss.

Instead of swinging randomly, US educational leaders can reimagine a reliable relationship with ethics and competency when it:

a. Depends on decision-making that employs scholarship and understands that "why a leader is effective requires that we examine how different behaviors interact in a mutually consistent way" (Yukl, 2012, p. 76).
b. Puts de-development (Nutt, 2004) into action to craft what "Peter Levine describes [as] relational politics or the 'interactions among people who make decisions or take collective actions knowing something about one another's ideas, preferences, and interests' (2014, para. 9)" (Knight Abowitz, 2018, p. 12).
c. Ensures that educational leadership is authentic behavior chosen from a knowledge, human relations, and research base. Yukl (2012) provides a sketch for this understanding of the value of a comprehensive understanding about leadership behaviors chosen from a mix of research, experience, and lived experience.

IS LEADERSHIP A PATTERN-SEEKING DEVICE?

The human brain has long been understood as a pattern-seeking device (Lowery, 1998). Educators look for, identify, teach, and evaluate patterns. For example, classroom instruction that engages students—cognitively, emotionally, behaviorally—with comparing the styles of two artists, the prose of two authors, or the political priorities of two presidents builds a habit of mind, a thinking skill that facilitates pattern-seeking. From the perspective of a teacher, formative evaluation is pattern-seeking in student learning about what's been taught.

Pattern-seeking—identifying patterns and reflecting about patterns—is leadership *sensitivity*. Sensitivity, in this case, "concerns likelihood of noticing occasions to engage in [a] behavior" (Perkins and Tishman, 2016). Researchers note that both *ability* (capacity to enact a behavior) and *inclination* (motivation to enact a behavior) precede sensitivity and are more likely than sensitivity. In fact, sensitivity is identified as "the chief bottleneck in effective intellectual performance" (Perkins and Tishman, 2016).

An argument central to this discussion is that educational leaders in US public schools generally have the ability and inclination to seek patterns that influence the effectiveness of educational environments on behalf of all students. But, this argument also incorporates the point that educational leaders often lack *sensitivity* and do not notice the multiple occasions for enacting reliable school leadership. Function, as this discussion will indicate, is the key that unlocks sensitivity for educational leadership.

Theories and Styles and Patterns, Oh My!

It could be argued that the multitude of theories about educational leadership constitute patterns and that these are the patterns that leaders can access and apply during their daily practice. But depending on this randomness to constitute a pattern is like depending on a Jackson Pollock painting to mirror the patterns of a Norman Rockwell painting.

Indeterminate, random, and disconnected, the diffuse quality of research and practice for educational leadership yields insensitive, unreliable school leadership. One way to understand this woebegone educational leadership is found in the observation that "there is little systematic research to identify situations where specific leadership behaviors are most likely to impact performance outcomes" (Yukl, 2012, p. 77).

Unfocused, detached, and inconsistent, leadership choices and behaviors forsake reliability in favor of leadership as a reaction. Once sensitivity is unavailable to educational leaders, coherence is neglected and randomness is favored with the result that educational leadership leaves to chance what educational environments provide to students.

WHAT SHOULD LEADERS KNOW TO SERVE ALL STUDENTS?

Students are the reason for public education in America's democracy and students are the reason that school leadership is important. For educational leadership to shed the impediments that forestall reliability, for school leadership to intend the development of student-centric environments, virtue is fostered when educators choose to enact several dispositions:

- *Lived Experience and Culture:* Every student comes to school equipped to learn. Lived experience, meaning-making, and natural thinking are capacities sufficient to build memory and to engage students with *how to think* (Swensson, Ellis, and Shaffer, 2019b). Culture (the attributes of family, race, ethnicity, nationality, and so on, alongside culture conveyed through social media) is omnipresent and enriches the pursuit of the moral obligation of public education.
- *Know What Works:* Teaching, learning, and leadership are not conducive to recipes. Students are not ingredients to be blended into instructional, behavioral, emotional, or cultural cake mixes. Rather, leaders know that "what works" is a matter of learning about and engaging in "'all aspects of school leadership [and] seeing them as interrelated rather than discrete actions performed out of context' (Perez et al., 2010, p. 218)" (Lehman, 2013, p. 122).
- *Norms Lead:* Ciulla et al. (2018) observe that "some philosophers have argued that the very idea of a leader is loaded with normative implications" (p. 5). Norms—for example, expectations for teaching and learning, imperatives about social justice and respect—are fostered in, by, and for leadership. The implications of these norms reside in relationships, interactions, and functions of public schools and school districts.

LOOKING AT THIS CHAPTER IN THE REARVIEW MIRROR

Looking back at this chapter, readers can consider and confront imperatives about leadership in our public schools. These imperatives include:

1. Second only to quality instruction in the classroom, school leadership has the most profound effect on the intellectual and emotional lives of students.

2. The complexity of school leadership cannot be underestimated.
3. Democracy in the United States depends on the civic engagement, self-efficacy, social justice, and fairness learned and expressed within the community of school established by educational leadership.
4. School leadership demands honest appraisal and continuous improvement of the educational environment that students experience.

The rearview mirror provided for every chapter throughout this book is an opportunity for reflection. Looking backward in this way, especially since reflection is a precious resource for leaders, allows readers to consider how what's been shared can be used to establish the future of educational leadership that all students deserve. For this chapter, the rearview mirror provides readers with a chance to gather their thoughts about these questions:

- Using this chapter as a foundation, what does this statement mean to you: "In educational administration, we believe that if there is a moral imperative for the profession, it is to serve the *'best interests of the student'*" (Stefkovich and Begley, 2007, p. 212).
- What will you do to avoid the inadequacies that prey on school leaders?
- How do you identify, seek, and apply patterns in your day-to-day school experiences? Explain whether pattern-seeking is a viable way to exercise reliable educational leadership.
- Where would you take your leadership (regardless of your current role) if you adopted the majority of the perspectives shared in this chapter?

Chapter 2

It's NOT All About You

> "Leadership is a fundamental part of the human condition and how we live and work together."
>
> —Ciulla, Knights, Mabey, and Tomkins, 2018, p. 1

This chapter is a cautionary tale. Evidence abounds of instances when a leader's hubris, a leader's belief in his/her infallibility, become leadership (Greenfield, 2004). Self-serving use of titles and positions speaks to a person's conviction that his or her needs and interests *are* leadership. These pseudo-leaders subvert the greater good of public education and earn an appropriate label for their approach: *narcissistic leadership* (Rosenthal and Pittinsky, 2006; Van Wart, 2013).

The dreadful mistake that narcissistic leaders make is to believe that leadership (its authority, responsibility, rewards, power, and glory) is all about them. Compounding this error, all-about-me-leadership places the responsibility for faults, errors, mistakes, and crises at the feet of anyone but the leader. "Research shows that an ethos celebrating individual achievement has been shoving aside other motivations, such as the drive to empower people, that are essential for successful leadership" (Spreier, Fontaine, and Malloy, 2006, p. 1).

Leadership theories tend to endow an individual with *positional leadership* (Wielkiewicz and Stelzner, 2005) simply because of a title or role in an organization. Scholars note that this is one type of *social construction* and that "positional leaders manipulate the context and constructions of their followers" (Wiekiewicz and Stelzner, 2005, pp. 327–328). Conventional wisdom portrays positional leaders "as being masculine, aggressive, rational, self-confident, competitive, dominant, task oriented, intelligent, and independent" (Wiekiewicz and Stelzner, 2005, p. 328).

Throughout this chapter, readers will be called to consider the obligations of leadership to goals, interactions, morality, and outcomes that are greater than themselves. Positional leadership, narcissistic leadership, charismatic leadership, or great-man leadership are all examples of leadership emerging from narrow and restrictive social construction.

All-about-me leadership and its failure to recognize virtue and service to a greater good will be examined in this chapter. Readers will encounter:

- The introduction of a syndrome that is the antithesis of the leadership that all students deserve.
- A discussion of leadership devoted to "mirror-gazing."
- The price paid when educational leadership ignores or forsakes the moral obligation of public education.

The gist of this cautionary tale is that self-centered leadership is alluring, inspiring, and transformative in all the wrong ways. This chapter's content is a warning about the ease with which school leaders can lose sight of their responsibilities and obligations to something bigger than they are.

AN INTERVENING NOTE

The authors are keenly aware of the tendency for critics to rivet their criticism to fixable, infrequent, and/or charade problems that arise in US public education. Therefore, as this chapter serves to caution educational leaders, it does so to set the stage for exploring the transformative practices and positive potential of school leadership. We are firm believers in the exceptional value, professionalism, and focus on students that most leaders in US public education enact daily.

Research findings speak to the positive impact of educational leadership and to the imperative for scholarship and practice that builds upon and extends the transformative effects of educational leadership. For instance, Hallinger's (2005) summary of research details the positive contributions of principals to "school effectiveness and student achievement indirectly through actions they take to influence school and classroom conditions (Hallinger and Heck, 1996a, b, 1999)" (p. 9).

Gutmann and Ben-Porath (2015) speak to two responsibilities at the center of public education in a democracy: "develop in young people both the knowledge and skills that individuals need to live free lives and the shared values . . . that citizens need to support the institutions that enable them to live freely" (p. 1). Virtuous educational leadership invests in the lives of students to transcend barriers to individual freedom.

The norm for public school leadership is ethical, dedicated, service. In the rare instances when those in positions of authority carry out their role unethically or immorally, leadership ceases to exist. The absence of virtue reveals the choices, decisions, and behaviors not of leaders but of tyrants, miscreants, or charlatans.

THE TROUBLED HISTORY OF EDUCATIONAL LEADERSHIP

The troubled history of educational leadership reveals the failure of scholars and practitioners to separate educational leadership from organizational leadership (Orazi, Turrini, and Valotti, 2013). Research identifies numerous, disparate, overlapping, applied, and/or theoretical styles, models, and/ or practices relevant to business and industry leadership that may or may not segue with what has been referred to as *public sector leadership*, which is synonymous with educational leadership (Orazi, Turrini, and Valotti, 2013).

As an example of public sector leadership, educational leadership cannot escape the troubles that afflict American history. US schools often reflect the worst inclinations and prejudices that pockmark our nation's history. Scholars confirm "the historical record which demonstrates that [school leaders] were defending racism, stereotypes of a people rooted in prejudice, and standing by an agenda of I.Q. testing anchored in eugenics" (English, 2005, p. 81).

Organizational Leadership First and Foremost

The influence of organizational leadership is unavoidable in the research and practice of educational leadership. For instance, studies about organizational leadership identify "achievement—meeting or exceeding a standard of excellence or improving personal performance—as one of three internal drivers . . . that explain how we behave" (Spreier, Fontaine, and Malloy, 2006, p. 2). The other two drivers are "affiliation—maintaining close personal relationships—and power, which involves being strong and influencing or having an impact on others" (Spreier, Fontaine, and Malloy, 2006, p. 2).

Like much of the research about organizational leadership, these "drivers" suggest that leadership is expressed by choices and behaviors born of an *all-about-me* approach. As Zucker (2019) observes, "efficiency that allow[s] highly task-focused leaders to be so productive often come[s] at the expense of a more people-based focus. Things like building relationships, inspiring a team, developing others, and showing empathy can fall by the wayside" (p. 2).

Virtue-Free Leadership

Dependent on theory emerging from the business world, then, educational leadership can have a tentative grip on virtue. A relatively recent phenomenon—privatization or choice schooling represented by charter schools and vouchers, among other mechanisms—illustrates that virtue-free school leadership is both possible and, in some instances, prevalent in the twenty-first century.

Free market theory was imported into public education in the late 1950s and received significant support after the publication of *A Nation at Risk* (1983). "The common thread running through programs born from *A Nation at Risk* has been to infuse the educational system with more businesslike accountability, to rely on data and metrics to drive success" (Rice, 2017, p. 56). This thread ties leadership of US schools to "a set of assumptions built on the economic definition of a public good that views education as only an individual experience sought to fulfill one's unique desires" (Knight Abowitz and Stitzlein, 2018, p. 34).

Aligned with free market theory, "schools are simply one kind of organization to be positioned in a market. In the pursuit of profit one examines any means to reduce variance. Differences are 'smoothed out'" (English, 2005, p. 92).

Virtue Kidnapped in the Free Market

Virtue-free education and the marketplace leadership that supports it are responsible for historic and egregious educational failures (Goldstein, 2015; Mayer, 2017; Suitts, 2019). Proponents of free market theory position various mechanisms (e.g., charter schools, vouchers, virtual education) to serve individual proclivities; reduce taxes for public school funding; sanction or eliminate entire schools; and undercut services to special needs, ELL, and gifted/talented students (Ravitch, 2020; Swensson and Shaffer, 2020).

Virtue is kidnapped in this market; there is no relationship between the needs of the market and the success of its customers. Markets are, above all else, amoral (Lubienski, 2013). Adherence to ideologies that rely on markets as if they have a relationship between ethics and competency enforce separation and singularity among US students. Data from Louisiana during the early 1960s, for instance, reveals that "all voucher-supported private schools were segregated by race—either all-white or all-black" (Suitts, 2019).

Standards: Meeting the Needs of the Educational Market

National standards seeped out of free market theory to ensure that teaching and learning are all about ideology while masquerading as the means to improve the academic proficiency of all students. Putting marketplace and other ideologies first in public education establishes enrollment segregation (Swensson, Ellis, and Shaffer, 2019a) while individual students are ignored en masse when data about standards provides pictures of large groups of students referred to as "cohorts." Ideologies and the outcomes they visit upon public schools via standardized testing "have become staples in the environment of America's schools (Fuhrman, Goertz, and Weinbaum, 2007; Lipman, 2004; Malen, 2003)" (Spillane, Parise, and Zoltners Sherer, 2011, p. 568).

Standards grew from the involvement of the National Council for the Accreditation of Teacher Education (NCATE) which spawned the Educational Leadership Constituency Council (ELCC) and both were supported by the National Alliance for Business and the Business Roundtable.

This cabal—augmented later during the twenty-first century by the American Legislative Exchange Council (ALEC) and other like-minded entities—stood behind the Business Roundtable and its development of "a plan for transforming public education involving nine essential components which involved the promulgation of standards, state wide testing, and accountability for results (Emery and Ohanian, 2004, p. 35)" (English, 2005, p. 94).

Public schools and educational leaders, meanwhile, are given little choice when it comes to whether to "buy" what's being marketed. For the most part, the only choice public educators have is to acquiesce to standards and the mandates that impose them. Few school leaders are in a position to act as true consumers in the virtue-free schooling market.

MIRROR, MIRROR, ON MY WALL: A LEADERSHIP SYNDROME

Students who use school lockers frequently put small mirrors inside the locker door. This symbol of an age-appropriate developmental characteristic of middle and high school students—the *universal audience*—is the opportunity students take to make sure they look good because they believe they are the star of a show that everyone is watching.

Unfortunately, some school leaders behave as if *they* deserve a universal audience. Some leaders enter their roles so enamored with themselves that their choices and behaviors form a barrier to virtuous leadership because their self-interest overwhelms service to others (Ciulla et al., 2018, p. 3).

Scholars refer to this as "pseudotransformational leadership. This term refers to leaders who are self-consumed, exploitive, and power-oriented, with warped moral values (Bass and Riggio, 2006)" (Northouse, 2007, p. 177). This term describes a transactional approach to choices, decisions, and behaviors in the sense that these leaders transact professional relationships on behalf of themselves.

Akin to the fairy tale villainess who asks a mirror to confirm her self-validating beauty, pseudotransformational leadership is self-aggrandizing tunnel vision. Referred to throughout this discussion as the *who's the greatest one of all* (WGOA) syndrome, this deficiency is an individual's myopia and a leadership plague.

THE ORIGINS OF EDUCATIONAL LEADERSHIP

To some degree, the catastrophes unleashed by the WGOA syndrome result from school leadership being taken for granted or misunderstood as a minor attribute of an educational environment. Northouse (2007) illustrates several of the mundane perceptions that facilitate leadership as self-aggrandizement: "the focus of group processes," "from a personality perspective," or "an act or behavior" (Northouse, 2007, p. 2). If leadership is perceived as no greater than these mundanities, the door to misanthropic, me-first, leading is left wide open.

Walking first through this portal is *classical bureaucratic theory*, the scholarly origin of organizational leadership. This theory is rooted in linear, hierarchical, leadership. Classical bureaucratic theory was adopted from studies of efficient business leadership by scholars and practitioners eager to establish a research-based understanding for the nature of educational leadership (Goldring and Greenfield, 2002).

Often the most recognizable feature of educational leadership from the early twentieth century to the present, classical bureaucratic theory cloaks school leaders in the grandiose notion that "they were no longer mere teachers. They were captains of industry (Button, 1966; Callahan and Button, 1964)" (Murphy et al., 2016, p. 262). "Images of the school as a rational-technical 'system of production' remain firmly embedded in the psyche of policy makers and pervade most educational reforms promulgated since the early 1980's" (Goldring and Greenfield, 2002, p. 2).

The misguided expressions within all-about-you leadership add to the morass of leadership examples that are "balkanized . . . clusters of theories and approaches" (Fernandez, 2005, p. 200).

THE COMMITMENTS OF AN EDUCATIONAL LEADER

The characteristics assigned to an educational leader often reflect the extent to which that leader is what others presuppose or expect about leadership. What people perceive when they identify leadership can be a confirmation of their own expectations that Eagly and Chin (2010) refer to as *subjective constructs*.

Subjective constructs are beliefs "that leaders are ambitious, confident, self-sufficient, and dominant, that is, well endowed with agentic and competent qualities (Powell, Butterfield, and Parent, 2002; Schein, 2001)" (Eagly and Chin, 2010, p. 217). How a leader construes his/her commitments to purpose, mission, and outcomes of public education leadership can boil down to currying favor with influential or powerful individuals whose subjective constructs establish non-negotiables for a leader.

Under these circumstances, a leader's commitments become a self-fulfilling prophecy for whatever "others" deem leadership to be. If subjective constructs are enforced as the expectations for school leadership or if school leaders anoint themselves with the WGOA syndrome, ineptitude, unethical conduct, or laissez-faire school involvement become possible and leadership becomes the pursuit of lesser goods.

To move beyond commitments to leadership as if it is an innate quality, or as if it is the WGOA syndrome, or as if it is the mirror image of expectations embedded in the perspectives of others, educational leadership during the remainder of the twenty-first century requires a reorientation initiated by a pair of commitments:

Commitment #1: Moral Obligation of Public Education

Reimagining how educational leadership is construed begins with a commitment to the moral obligation of public education.

Greenfield (2004) provides a two-pronged synthesis of the moral obligation of public education: first, educating the children of the public is inherently a moral endeavor, and second, "relationships among people are at the very center of the work of school administrators and teachers, and for this reason school leadership is, by its nature and focus, a moral activity (Foster, 1986; Hodgkinson, 1978, 1983, 1991; Starratt, 1991, 1996)" (p. 174).

Values that represent this obligation include "overarching principles [that] have been agreed on in our society and within the teaching profession—principles dealing with honesty, fairness, protection of the weak, and respect for all people (Clark, 1990, p. 252)" (Campbell, 2008, p. 602). As these principles illustrate, morality is about interactions that "focus on the effects those actions have upon the welfare of others" (Nucci, 2008, p. 294).

Because socialization is an inevitable part of education and because public education in the United States is a critical element in the equation of democracy, the moral obligation of public education is a commitment to ethics in school leadership.

Commitment #2: Poly-Collegial Leadership

Reimagining educational leadership requires, next, a commitment to discarding the notion that leadership is proprietary (Ciulla et al., 2018). Instead of sustaining the perception that educational leadership is "owned" by a title, existing in one individual, or designated on a staffing chart, school leadership must be understood as *poly-collegial*: all school staff lead.

All-in as a commitment of educational leadership is based on the understanding that "everyone has a moral obligation to be actively engaged in the world" (Ciulla et al., 2018, p. 9). The moral obligation of public education fueled by intentional leadership at the building level, for example, influences the "leadership provided by many possible sources—individual teachers, staff teams, parents, central office staff, students and vice principals—as well as the principal" (Leithwood, Harris, and Hopkins, 2008, p. 34).

The moral obligation of public education, crafted by positive leadership, is oriented as "a collective construct that can be distributed among teachers and support staff (Gronn and Hamilton, 2004; Spillane et al., 2007) through the cultivation of relationships and networks (Fullan, 2001)" (Jacobson, 2011, p. 35). This commitment is a "sense of coordinated purpose" (Jacobson, 2011, p. 36) evinced in decisions and behaviors among colleagues.

The Conjunction of Leadership Commitments: *Leading-Out*

The root word of education means *lead-out* (Swensson, Ellis, and Shaffer, 2019b; Swensson and Shaffer, 2020). Virtue in educational leadership sustains the commitment to lead-out the values of the moral obligation of public education including "honesty, a sense of fairness, integrity, compassion, patience, respect, impartiality, care, dedication, and other such core virtues" (Campbell, 2008, p. 603).

This commitment unto itself leads-out educators to a commitment to the primary purpose of public education: engaging all students with the capacities and habits of mind/thinking skills that constitute *how to think* (Swensson, Ellis, and Shaffer, 2019a; Swensson and Shaffer, 2020). This primary purpose of public education facilitates the futures of all students as it engenders student capacities to choose and express the values of moral purpose in relationship to the principles of social justice.

A Reimagining of Educational Leadership

These commitments spark a demand that educational leadership become more than it is. Educational leadership is responsible for functioning on behalf of commitments that are greater than any one person. The educational leadership that all students deserve rests in

> the disposition to draw out student capacities to fulfill education's moral obligation [that] lies in the original power of teaching and learning to establish connections "between reasoning and social conventions and moral concepts about fairness and human welfare." (Nucci, 2008, p. 292)

Scholars opine that leaders, ultimately, must make a commitment to taking responsibility (Ciulla et al., 2018). Taking responsibility is facilitated when educators employ reflection to develop, renew, and expand their knowledge and learning.

THE GREATER GOOD AND EDUCATIONAL LEADERSHIP

Educational leadership is a commitment to the greater good. The scope of this greater good is illuminated when Ciulla et al. (2018) recall that Plato identifies "one of the key normative aspects of leadership when he argues that it is about pursuing the interests of others or of a cause" (p. 3).

Public educators continue to take responsibility for this norm amidst "the uncertainty, turbulence, messiness, and unpredictability of the milieu of schooling, and the essentially 'people-changing' goals of schools" (Goldring and Greenfield, 2002, p. 2). The interests of others or of a cause (e.g., the principles of democracy) provide a gyroscope with which educational leadership can balance professional function on behalf of reliability in US traditional public education.

Too many factors, however, delay or obstruct the pursuit of a greater good. Discursive scholarship and hit-or-miss professional behaviors render educational leadership unreliable. Amidst pressures to conform to external mandates and expectations, and without a coherent sense of how leadership establishes educational environments that all students deserve, leadership reliability—the capacity to perform well consistently—is lost in many schools and school districts.

A Coda to This Cautionary Tale

If this cautionary tale about educational leadership were put to music, these next few paragraphs would be a coda: concluding the tale but adding a necessary, slightly different, direction to the music.

The coda to this cautionary note means acknowledging Van Wart's (2013) observation that most types of leadership "can lead to lower productivity and effectiveness if not managed effectively (Goodsell, 2011; McGuire, 2006)" (p. 559). This significant problem arises, in part, from the "conceptual fuzziness" (Goldring and Greenfield, 2002, p. 1) of the abundant scholarship meant to inform educational leadership.

Worse, management *is* the frequent response to this conceptual fuzziness. Rationality and efficiency constitute a conditioned response to difficulties that attend leadership in the indeterminate zone.

Fuzziness is responsible for the often random, unfocused, and divergent practices developed from the abundant literature about leadership theories and styles. This cornucopia mimics the overwhelming selection that shoppers encounter in the snack foods aisle at the supermarket. Research about leadership offers row upon row of chips and candies that are enticing and tasty but that offer little to nurture educational leadership as a reliable function. Management is a façade behind which educational leadership is little more than sugar, fat, and an expiration date that's two years old.

It should come as no surprise that too few school leaders know how to bring reliability to their professional practice. Certainly, the influence of leadership varies from school to school and from leader to leader because professional relationships, school context, external influences, and numerous other factors are variable. But, too often the vagaries of circumstance are a convenient excuse for leadership that does not live up to its potential.

The potential of educational leadership is found when leaders exert direct, intentional influence on school attributes and outcomes. Leaders exert a substantive influence on the commitment of colleagues, the depth of staff morale, the effects associated with school organization, and the obligations, responsibilities, and morality engendered by school ethos (Moore, 2009, p. 23).

The chasm between the potential for and the practice of reliable educational leadership is the point at which this coda makes its turn. Establishing educational leadership with the capacity to pursue the greater good reliably requires an intentional approach to the primary purpose for and the moral obligation of public education.

Scholars provide cues about the nature of this approach to school leadership. "Integrative frameworks incorporate leadership skills, traits, behaviors, and styles and situational variables in a single theoretical model to explain the effectiveness of a leader (Hunt, 1991; Yukl, 2002)" (Fernandez, 2005, p. 200). Several concepts imply the intentionality of reliable educational leadership. These are shared in textbox 2.1 and will be explored later in this discussion.

TEXTBOX 2.1 FOUNDATIONAL ELEMENTS OF FUNCTIONAL EDUCATIONAL LEADERSHIP

Leith, the root word of leadership: This root word "literally means to step across a threshold—and to let go of whatever might limit stepping forward" (Senge, Hamilton, and Kania, 2015, p. 2).

Agency: Agency is referred to as "free will," "knowing right and wrong," "soul," "fault," "sin," "authorship," "praise," "addressee," "respondent," and so on (Matusov, von Duyke, and Kayumova, 2016, p. 422).

Virtue: The nature of educational leadership and the relationships that comprise it shift when "virtue or *arête* is an excellence that encompasses both ethics and competency" (Ciulla, et al., 2018, p. 5). Virtue constitutes the shared vision of *the good* necessary and sufficient to the competencies or functions of reliable educational leadership.

Primary purpose of public education: The primary purpose of public education is engaging all students with the capacities and habits of mind/thinking skills that constitute *how to think* (Swensson, Ellis, and Shaffer, 2019b; Swensson and Shaffer, 2020).

Adaptive challenges: Douglass (2018) calls *adaptive challenges* which "are problems for which there is not an existing or predefined solution" (p. 388). Adaptive challenges are found in controversies, societal problems, professional disagreements, and a host of other dilemmas that confront educators daily.

Ecological systems theory: ecological systems theory (Bronfenbrenner, 1979). Scholars indicate that this contribution to scholarship "is presented as a theory of human development in which everything is seen as interrelated and our knowledge of development is bounded by context, culture, and history" (Darling, 2007, p. 204).

Emergent process: Wielkiewicz and Stelzner (2005) who indicate that "our definition of leadership is that of an *emergent process;* that is, it emerges from the interactions and actions of individuals within an ecological system" (p. 330).

Process: "Northouse uses the word 'process' to describe how leaders influence because the word implies an interaction; that is, leaders 'affect and are affected by' those they lead" (Abrahams, 2007, p. 87). The reciprocal nature of influence means that leadership as *active person* is dialectical and multi-relational.

Functional educational leadership: functional educational leadership will guide the remainder of this discussion: *educational leadership is a professional function exercised through interaction between cognition and behavior chosen within the context of a school community to create, sustain, and improve the educational environment that all students deserve.*

Although a mere conglomeration of research about educational leadership invites a comparison with rearranging deck chairs on the *Titanic*, postmodern social construction implies that school leaders must "embrace difference and diversity because each construction that lies outside the typical or the normal opens the door for greater understanding of something that was previously not perceived and therefore not understood" (Sackney and Mitchell, 2002, p. 891).

Educational leaders have not understood that the age-old acknowledgement of "leadership [as] a process whereby an individual influences a group of individuals to achieve a common goal" (Northouse, 2007, p. 3) means little in the pursuit of the greater good without an understanding of how to ensure that this overarching function of leadership is reliable. To this end, a comprehensive understanding of reliability becomes the paradigm necessary and sufficient for conceptualizing and practicing educational leadership that all students deserve during the remainder of the twenty-first century.

LOOKING AT THIS CHAPTER IN
THE REARVIEW MIRROR

This chapter issues a warning to prospective and current school leaders: leadership that is "all about you" is neither service to something greater nor creation of learning environments that all students deserve. Choosing behaviors that represent the *who's the greatest one of all* syndrome is an investment in short-sighted and selfish decisions that ignore the wealth of potential in school leadership while denying that educational leadership has any purpose other than self-aggrandizement.

Several questions are posed here to allow the reader to gather her/his thoughts about how best to avoid self-aggrandizing leadership that sells short students, colleagues, and communities:

- Based on your experiences with leaders in schools and school districts, describe the decisions and behaviors that they made indicating that their leadership was NOT all about them.
- Based on your experiences with leaders in schools and school districts, describe the decisions and behaviors that they made indicating that their leadership WAS all about them.
- Why do leaders think that WGOA, the syndrome described in this chapter, constitutes viable professional behavior?
- What will you do to ensure that your leadership is never all about YOU?

Chapter 3

I Don't Think I've Ever Seen So Many Trees

There are times when a person concentrates so completely on a single idea that other relevant ideas are almost invisible. When this happens, it is said that the person fixated on the one idea *can't see the forest for the trees*.

As it turns out, the study and practice of educational leadership often represent an intense focus on individual trees—for example, the theories and styles generated by research—instead of a perspective about a more comprehensive, interconnected, and functioning school leadership. The purpose of this chapter is to examine how single concepts about educational leadership obscure the interrelated reliable leadership that all students deserve in US public schools.

In this chapter, *old growth* and *second growth* theories are explored for the insights they provide about educational leadership. Although these insights, and the knowledge that supports them, are concepts that can shed light on select characteristics of educational leadership, these notions offer little to facilitate the reliable function of educational leadership.

At present, practitioners and scholars vie to identify their favorite examples of educational leadership, decry the unsuitability of theories or practices that differ, and/or cultivate "boutique" labels, styles, or theories. This scholarly and practical traffic jam symbolizes the disorienting effect of conceptually fuzzy thinking about educational leadership in which "sometimes different terms are used to refer to the same type of behavior, and sometimes the same term is used for different forms of behavior" (Yukl, 2012, p. 66).

As a result, educational leadership is often perceived as the embodiment of any of several stand-alone labels (e.g., instructional leadership, servant leadership) that encourage perseveration on individual trees instead of the forest that stands all around (Van Wart, 2013).

This chapter leaves to other resources (see English, 2006, vols. 1 and 2) an exhaustive examination of the singular visions of educational leadership. Instead, this chapter explores how representative theories are identified as if they are educational leadership. During this encounter, readers will acquire a vantage point from which to understand:

1. The precursors that school leaders need to consider before taking on any leadership role.
2. The *old growth*, *second growth*, and *in the weeds* theories and concepts about educational leadership.
3. Research suggests that leadership in US public education ought to be a forest.
4. A metaphor for how practitioners and scholars are entangled by educational leadership.
5. The *indeterminate zone* of educational leadership.

EDUCATIONAL LEADERSHIP: TREE IDENTIFICATION

So many trees! Stand-alone notions about educational leadership include styles, skills, theories, types, practices, and models. From a practitioner's point of view, the tasks of leadership can be simplified if they align with one stand-alone notion or another. Further, many of the single theories and styles are identified as the leadership *skills* that arise "from a relatively managerial perspective, mentoring aspect or organizational change approach" (Van Wart, 2013, p. 554).

In some instances, educational leadership is identified as a unique *style*. For example, "Hunt (1996) described three styles of leadership—direct, organizational, and systems." *Directing style*, *coaching style*, and *delegating style* are singled out by Hersey and Blanchard (Van Wart, 2013, p. 556). In addition, theorists identify six styles of business leadership including *visionary*, *coaching*, *affiliative*, *democratic*, *pacesetting*, and *commanding* (Goleman, Boyatzis, and McKee, 2004).

Always eager to fixate on new trees, scholars use various modifiers including *participatory*, *supportive*, or *achievement-oriented* (Van Wart, 2013, p. 557) to further differentiate among similar leadership labels. For example, behaviors associated with leadership such as decision-making are broken down into unique, separate, categories such as *autocratic or directive*; *consultative*; *collaborative or joint*; and *delegating* (Van Wart, 2013, p. 557).

The Pitfalls of Educational Leadership

Educational leadership is understood and practiced as if it's a singular construct. Allegiance to any one brand-name notion of leadership is a trap. Several pitfalls and foibles accompany present-day leadership singularities:

- Leaders cannot see the totality of educational leadership without substantial knowledge about the constructs, goals, behaviors, and outcomes derived from leadership theories and the practices associated with them. Missing the forest for the trees is a fundamental dilemma for leaders in any profession or business. Ignorance about the reciprocal relationships among trees within a forest* isolates a leader. Too often, educational leadership is as isolated as a maple tree in a planter devoid of interconnectivities facilitated by function, mutuality, and virtue.

    [*Authors' note: Richard Powers (2018) provides a sterling exploration of the botanical relationships among and between trees in forests in his book, *Overstory*. Powers' scientific insights about relationships among trees within a forest represents a metaphorical rationale for a reimagining of educational leadership.]
- Leadership is not a checklist. Nevertheless, school leaders too often resort to listing to meet expectations, standards, and/or evaluation processes. Murphy et al. (2016) illustrate how the evaluation of educators conducted with lists of standards mimic the historic implementation of time-motion studies that evaluated worker efficiency in industry. These lists calibrate leadership without regard to context, without regard to vendor-origination or ideological alignment, and without apology for representing the complexity of educational leadership—the forest—as if it's a census that counts one tree.
- Leadership does not exist, although it may have its name called, in the absence of integrity, honesty, ethical behavior, and fairness. Individuals who aspire to leadership in education, regardless of title or role, must determine always to be ethical. Leadership is both service and sacrifice on behalf of the greater good.
- Leadership embodies the last line of the time-honored epigram: *You can't please all the people all the time*. Leadership is not playing to the crowd, listening to the last, loudest voice, feathering your own nest, or speaking only subservience to power.
- Leaders, "regardless of where they reside in the organization or when and how they enact leadership, will often confront the ambiguous, the fragmented, the unexpected, and perhaps the unwanted" (Sackney and Mitchell, 2002, p. 898). The inability to engage with these indicators of

disorder, confusion, and chaos is an inability to summon virtue into school leadership.

OLD GROWTH, SECOND GROWTH, AND THE WEEDS

Old growth educational leadership includes the "traditional notions of leadership [that] focus on individuals who inhabit formal positions of power, and possess traits such as assertiveness, decisiveness, control, and domination (Fletcher, 2004)" (Douglass, 2018, p. 388). Like the oldest, never-harvested trees in a forest, old growth educational leadership ideas tower over the practices of school leaders.

Old Growth Educational Leadership

Old growth theories spawned the study of educational leadership. These continue to influence, sometimes dominate, the practices of school leaders:

- *Scientific management* (associated with Frederick Taylor and his scholarship that spanned the decades between the early 1900s and the late 1940s): "effective management requires planning, organizing, staffing, directing, coordinating, reporting, and budgeting, among other things (Gulick and Urwick, 1937)" (Van Wart, 2013, p. 444).
- *Classical bureaucratic theory* (associated with Henri Fayol, early 1900s): Fayol offered precepts for efficient management as guidelines meant for the success of upper echelon managers in industry and business.
- *Human relations/Organizational behavior theory* (associated with Elton Mayo and his *Hawthorne Studies*, late 1930s): Although Mayo's original study intended to add to existing scholarship about efficient leadership in industry, his work created an opening for scholarship to inquire about the needs of workers and the effects of the organization on employees (Cordiero and Cunningham, 2013; Owens and Valesky, 2011).

None of this early scholarship was meant to describe or explain leadership in the realm of public schools. Nevertheless, these studies and their implications influenced thinking about educational leadership because educational leaders and scholars were keen to develop a scholarly purview about educational leadership. The theories about business leadership tied to efficiencies, profit-motives, and top-down management were given a school-yard spin and became lenses through which scholars and practitioners began to see management or administration as the essence of efficient educational leadership.

As management and leadership become schoolhouse synonyms, the hierarchical ethos and step-by-step agency associated with business and industry emerged as the calling card for school leadership (DeMatthews, 2014). "Management theorists have regarded behaviors such as competing with peers, imposing wishes on subordinates, and behaving assertively as prototypical of the managerial role (Miner, 1993)" (Eagly and Chin, 2010, p. 217).

Second Growth Educational Leadership

Alongside old growth notions, *second growth* theories about educational leadership sprouted. Research expanded; new theories about educational leadership multiplied. For instance, during the 1960s and 1970s, three points of scholarly focus about educational leadership included "leadership traits, skills, and styles, the two-factor theory encompassing initiating structure and consideration, and the concepts of situational leadership and contingency theory" (Greenfield, 2004, p. 176).

Second growth concepts represent a wide range of leadership labels generated in hopes of advancing knowledge and practice relevant to school leadership:

Adaptive leadership: Senge, Hamilton, and Kania (2015) speak to adaptive leadership as the means by which leaders alter institutional and other conditions for subordinates who are having difficulties (p. 2). The alteration of these conditions is leadership that fosters collective learning by those seeking to eradicate the problem.

Applied critical leadership: Santamaria and Santamaria (2015) identify applied critical leadership as "an example of culturally responsive leadership in education where the practice is drawn from positive attributes of a leader's identity (Santamaria and Santamaria, 2012)" (p. 22).

Collaborative leadership: Collaborative leadership is identified not only as "power sharing among organizations (e.g., Crosby and Bryson, 2010; Newell, Reeher, and Ronayne, 2012)" (Van Wart, 2013, p. 559) but also as "sharing decision-making responsibility among a broader group of stakeholders (creating) legitimacy for collective decisions about instructional priorities" (Wahlstrom and Seashore Louis, 2008, p. 483). Hallinger and Heck (2010) list empowering staff and students, facilitating extensive involvement in decision-making, and establishing school-wide accountability for learning in their discussion of this type of leadership.

Comprehensive school reform (CSR): Comprehensive school reform is what scholars describe as the *third wave* of school reform fostered by the publication of *A Nation at Risk* (1983) that "focused on overcoming the limitations associated with piece-meal attempts to improve schools (Desimone, 2002)" (Klar and Brewer, 2013, p. 6).

Contingency leadership: This theory states that depending on the situation, such as the task to be accomplished, and the composition of the group to perform the task, a leader selects whether to take a more task-oriented, managerial, or controlled approach or a relationship-oriented, transformational, or shared approach (Urick and Bowers, 2014, p. 123).

Continuous improvement leadership: Closely related to instructional leadership, leadership riveted to continuous improvement is "the ability to positively impact instructional guidance, professional capacity, school-community connections, and a student-focused environment" (Murphy et al., 2016, p. 259).

Distributed leadership: Bennett (2003) is recognized for capturing the three defining characteristics of distributed leadership as "an emergent property of a group or network of interacting individuals exhibiting 'openness of boundaries', where the varieties of expertise are distributed across the many, not the few" (p. 7) (Latta, 2019, p. 76).

Other scholars identify three distinct forms of distribution of leadership: coordinated, collaborative, and collective (Latta, 2019). Van Wart (2013) indicates that distributive leadership is also known as *horizontal leadership* (p. 558). Latta (2019) found that "all forms of distributed leadership were shown to require both interdependence and involvement of group members" (p. 91).

Instructional leadership: Hopkins (2003) indicates that instructional leadership is "an approach" that leaders employ to ensure that teachers' behaviors are focused on student growth (p. 58).

System leadership: Senge, Hamilton, and Kania (2015) create a discussion about system leadership which is "able to bring forth collective leadership" (p. 27). These scholars introduce this construct as a perspective about leadership that recognizes that "we are at the beginning of the beginning in learning how to catalyze and guide systemic change at a scale commensurate with the scale of the problems we face, and all of us see but dimly" (Senge, Hamilton, and Kania, 2015, p. 28).

Transactional leadership: Transactional leadership constitutes a simple exchange of one thing for another: jobs for votes in the case of a political leader and the electorate; a congenial working atmosphere and security in return for keeping central office, parents and students happy in the case of a principal and teaching staff (Beare, Caldwell, and Millikan, 1989, p. 106).

Urick (2016) indicates that principals engage in transactional leadership when they "manage budgets, hire and supervise teachers, maintain safety and facilities" (pp. 152–153).

Transformational leadership: Urick and Bowers (2014) indicate that transformational leadership "is often measured by the degree that a principal communicates a mission, encourages development, and builds community" (p. 99). In both transformational leadership and LMX (leader-member exchange), the emotional sensitivity of a leader is highlighted. This sensitivity is at the core of the component of transformational leadership referred to as *individualized consideration* which "refers to the transformational leader's ability to be aware of specific follower feelings and needs and to be responsive to them (Bass and Riggio, 2006)" (Riggio and Reichard, 2008, p. 174).

Educational Leadership Down in the Weeds

Studies dedicated to old and second growth leadership can be organized into three broad categories of leader behaviors—task-oriented, relations-oriented, and development-oriented. As this trio implies, research from the 1980s and 1990s "failed to identify a definitive set of essential leadership behaviors" (Fernandez, 2005, pp. 198–199). Perhaps out of frustration with this situation, scholars took research about educational leadership deep into the scholarly and practical weeds.

Going to ground in this way continued the tradition of a scholarly and practical focus on singular constructs for educational leadership. During the last sixty years, research and commentary about leadership discovered "path-goal theory (House, 1971), leadership substitutes theory (Kerr and Jermier, 1978), situational leadership theory (Hersey and Blanchard, 1977), and the managerial grid (Blake and Mouton, 1964)" (Yukl, 2012, p. 69).

Attempts to improve practice somewhere in this definitional and theoretical undergrowth led to studies of site-based management, community-led schools, teacher empowerment (Hallinger, 2005); Theory X, Theory Y, and Theory Z (Cordeiro and Cunningham, 2013); full-service schools (Goldring and Greenfield, 2002); and Total Quality Management** (Deming, 1989; Larsson and Vinberg, 2010). Additional forays into the weeds identified choices for educational leadership including emotional leadership (Murphy et al., 2016); authentic leadership (Stefkovich and Begley, 2007); and collaborative leadership (Hallinger and Heck, 2010).

[**Authors' note: Within TQM, leadership per se is subordinated to a *factor* in the regimentation and tunnel-vision of data production and data manipulation that is prized in the TQM management model (Larsson and Vinberg, 2010).]

MANAGEMENT AS PRODUCT

"Sanction-heavy policy levers are frequently used among legislators as fallback solutions for complex social issues such as education (Mintrop and

Trujillo, 2005)" (Daly, 2009, p. 171). These levers manipulate the machinery that grinds up the trees and weeds of educational research and practice. Extruded from the machinery is management, the fallback product produced in lieu of leadership.

Management is a focus on regimentation and order that substitutes for coherence, mutuality, and the greater good. "Management is about coping with complexity; it brings order and predictability to a situation. . . . Leadership, then, is about learning how to cope with rapid change" (Kotter, 2011, p. 39). Management is the square peg of order and hierarchy hammered into the round hole of complex relationships, decisions, behaviors, and interconnectivities.

EDUCATIONAL LEADERSHIP IS STUCK

Well before the digital age, one of the toys that enthralled children—it was truly a simpler time—was a small flexible paper tube made with a herring bone pattern. By sticking one finger in each end of the tube and pulling in opposite directions, a child made the tube tighten around each finger. Getting both fingers unstuck became the fun frustration of this diversion.

US public education and educational leadership also are stuck but it's no fun. Scholars are stuck in one end of the tube of educational leadership without a comprehensive understanding of this construct. Practitioners are stuck in the other end unable to extract reliable daily leadership practice. The result, just like that paper tube toy, is that pulling in opposite directions yields only frustration. The compulsion to pull ceaselessly with the inevitable result that educational leadership cannot escape is tied to:

Assumptions about Charisma. The oldest notion about educational leadership that a "great man" and charisma are the wellspring of quality school leadership. "Charismatic leaders use their ability to express emotions to rouse and motivate followers and to build strong emotional ties with them" (Riggio and Reichard, 2008, p. 172). Although charisma has been debunked as a meaningful form of leadership, the tendency to identify the personality of an individual as leadership endures and is referred to as *emotional contagion* (Riggio and Reichard, 2008, p. 173).

The Conundrum of Change. Perhaps the most seductive assumption about educational leadership is that its purpose is to create change. In the early 1960s, "Lipham (1964, p. 122) focused exclusively on change when he defined leadership as 'the initiation of a new structure or procedure for accomplishing an organisation's goals and objectives'" (Beare, Caldwell, and Millikan, 1989, p. 101).

Present-day scholars reinforce the connection between leadership and change. Douglass (2018) conveys the tendency to see change as synonymous with school leadership when she writes that "this study defines leadership as a process of influencing positive change to achieve a desired goal or generate a new solution to a problem (Douglass, 2017)" (Douglass, 2018, p. 388).

Checklist Mania. Standards, encased in long lists of domains, principles, qualities, and other indicators of expectations for leaders, tend to be research-based blueprints for leadership that seek the well-being and academic success of students (Minkos et al., 2017). Some scholars indicate that "leadership is a set of learned practices that can be employed by any individual willing to make a difference" (Quin, Deris, Bischoff, and Johnson, 2015, p. 74). But applying a learned set of practices does not give school leaders the wherewithal to establish strong academic achievement for US students (Swensson, Ellis, and Shaffer, 2019a, pp. 102–103).

Theoretical Overlap. Scholars suggest that styles of leadership overlap (Urick and Bowers, 2014) and that this overlap may constitute the core of educational leadership. But, overlap of one style or theory of leadership with others is a confusion of its own kind. Spreier, Fontaine, and Malloy (2006) identify six styles of leadership and, in so doing, indicate that "there is no one best style of leadership" (p. 4).

Latta (2019) puts the dysfunction generated by overlap in stark profile in his description of distributed leadership:

> Distributed leadership has emerged as a distinct approach to collective leadership differing from shared (Pearce and Sims, 2000), emergent (Seers, 1996), team (Hulpia, Devos, and van Keer, 2010), and co-leadership in the degree to which it describes processes that occur outside the context of a pre-defined group. (Friedrich et al., 2009, p. 76)

Overlap is fostered, for example, when Urick and Bowers (2014) array three leadership behaviors—transformational leadership, instructional leadership, and shared instructional leadership—as the core set of behaviors that evince effective leadership. Other scholars identify a combination of transformational and transactional leadership (Orazi, Turrini, and Valotti, 2013).

In still more research, scholars envision a baklava of theoretical overlap in which "*transformational leadership* is a precursor for a distributed (Harris, 2004; Spillane et al., 2004) or shared form of *instructional leadership* (Marks and Printy, 2003; Printy et al., 2009)" (Urick and Bowers, 2014, p. 101).

Dysfunctional Goal-Setting. As Hallinger and Heck (2002) point out, goal-setting in educational leadership has been advanced as a rational and logical approach to measuring the effectiveness of a school or school district. But not only does research suggest that organizational and individual intensity dim after a goal is achieved but scholarship notes that educators also are bombarded by multiple, changing, goals whose half-life can be short.

"While goal-based approaches meet the organization's need for accountability, goal setting often fails to inspire people to meet a more fundamental need—to act" (Hallinger and Heck, 2002, p. 24). Research speaks to inaction as a primary facet of present-day educational leadership by indicating that "no significant difference exist(s) in the leadership practices of principals in low performing and high performing schools" (Quin et al., 2015, p. 73). Discursive and disconnected visions and versions of school leadership tend to make action or agency on behalf of robust student learning a hit-or-miss proposition.

The individual is the sequoia upon which inordinate attention is lavished by research about educational leadership. Singular, separate, alone, the individual is the apex of leadership identified through a literature review conducted on behalf of the American Educational Research Association (AERA). The AERA Task Force on Educational Leadership produced a report in which educational leadership is defined as "those persons who provide direction and exert influence in order to achieve the schools goals (Leithwood and Reihl, 2003, p. 9)" (Daly, 2009, p. 176).

IS THERE A FOREST AMONG THOSE TREES?

Trees and forests are metaphors that symbolize a persistent problem throughout the realm of educational leadership: fixation on one theory, style, or practice without regard for the greater good and function of the ecology that is a forest. Too many perceptions about educational leadership ignore the potential impact, magnitude, and value of the forest.

Instead of implementing brand-name theory or installing management models, some scholars envision educational leadership without resorting to buying into one product or another. Eagly and Chin (2010), for example, illustrate that "scholars of leadership have increasingly emphasized the effective leadership emerges from inspiring, motivating, and mentoring followers" (p. 219).

Some research permits glimpses of the forest. For example, scholars identify *integrated leadership* "that exhibited both transformational and shared instructional leadership" (Urick and Bowers, 2014, p. 103). Integrated leadership is also perceived as "frameworks [that] incorporate leadership skills, traits, behaviors, and styles and situational variables in a single theoretical model to explain leadership effectiveness" (Fernandez, 2005, p. 198).

In addition, Greenfield (2004) refers to a *dominant paradigm* for understanding and undertaking school leadership. The elements of this paradigm are "that organizational goals shape member behaviors and motives; that social systems concepts mirror the experience of participants; that bureaucratic structures guide behavior; [and] that decision making is a systematic process" (Greenfield, 2004, p. 177).

The Forest: Functional Educational Leadership

Identifying trees is one thing; understanding the presence and value of a forest is another thing entirely. There are limitless numbers of discrete ideas and a few frameworks that tie together one or two notions about educational leadership. Endless tree identification—leadership affixed to a scholarly label; leadership in pursuit of one strand or another of research—fails to acknowledge the greater good of leadership enacted from the whole, the forest, of scholarship, practice, and context.

To see the forest, to enact educational leadership, then, requires a perspective rooted in the understanding "that leadership is actually an *emergent* process. Emergence is defined as properties of a system that 'arise from the interactions and relationships among the parts' (Capra, 1996, p. 29)" (Wielkiewicz and Stelzner, 2005, p. 330). Understanding educational leadership in this way reveals the forest, a holistic, comprehensive, and intentional enactment of educational leadership that will be referred to throughout this discussion as *functional educational leadership*.

Functional educational leadership takes advantage of the reality that "leadership seems to be a gestalt phenomenon; greater than the sum of its parts" (Beare, Caldwell, and Millikan, 1989, p. 102). Functional educational leadership takes a cue from Capper and Green (2013) who observe that study of organizational theories "demands a 'creative act' from the student, to intellectually dig deep in the direct study of the theories and in the critical reflection about the theories as it relates to their practice" (p. 63).

EDUCATIONAL LEADERSHIP IN THE INDETERMINATE ZONE

Wondering about the nature of educational leadership is hardly a new phenomenon. Greenfield (2004), for instance, calls attention to a study from the 1960s that was "rooted in a controversy regarding the proper role of the school administrator: to provide routine administrative support versus to try to influence teachers' performance" (p. 175). The complexities, controversies, and conundrums inherent in present-day school leadership make this sixty-year-old dichotomy sound quaint.

Anything but quaint are the adaptive challenges (Wielkiewicz and Stelzner, 2005; Douglass, 2018) that confront educators daily. Adaptive challenges "are problems for which there is not an existing or predefined solution" (Douglass, 2018, p. 388). These challenges require, as Wielkiewicz and Stelzner (2005) illustrate, an ecological approach because "adaptive challenges require fundamental shifts in organizational expertise and the development of new, untried, experimental ways of adapting to a fundamentally changing environment" (p. 332). The preponderance of the professional work of school leaders in the twenty-first century must address adaptive challenges. This renders fixation on any one leadership theory, or on management instead of leadership, the progenitors of unreliability.

School leaders often find themselves in the middle when adaptive challenges develop in controversies, societal problems, professional disagreements, and a host of other dilemmas that walk in the schoolhouse door. The present-day disconnected and dysfunctional state of educational leadership results, as illustrated in figure 3.1, from its location in an *indeterminate zone*.

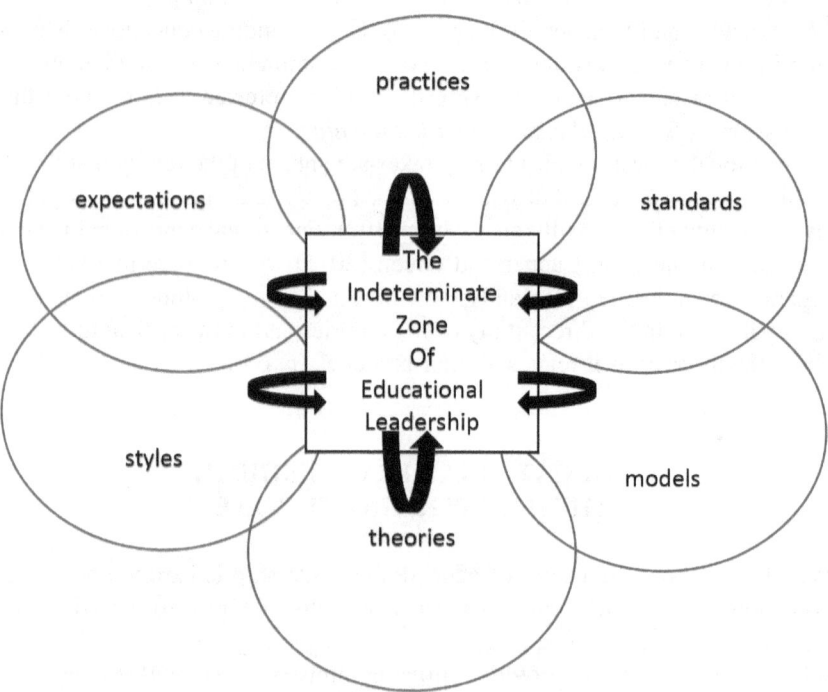

Figure 3.1 *Source:* Author created.

Extracting educational leadership from this zone is necessary if the promise and potential of the greater good served by leadership are to be fulfilled. The comprehensive functions of a forest imply the nature of the leadership required to engage all US students with the learning environments and school experiences that they deserve.

LOOKING AT THIS CHAPTER IN THE REARVIEW MIRROR

The blizzard of ideas that swirl around educational leadership are one reason that school leadership cannot be portrayed as the implementation of a leader's favorite theory or a "greatest hits" amalgam of selected research and practice. The limitless theories, styles, and notions about educational leadership leave the practice of school leadership trapped in a zone where professional practice is rendered indeterminate.

Several questions arise from the discussion in this chapter that will allow readers to engage their own perspectives:

- Should educational leadership be dependent on research-generated labels, theories, and attributes? Explain how you arrived at your answer and how your answer will affect your leadership.
- Why are there so many ideas about the nature of educational leadership?
- Based on your professional experiences, is it possible to craft school leadership that all students deserve and which aspects of this chapter influenced your answer?
- Are there ideas in this chapter that you would prioritize and are there ideas in this chapter that you would ignore when you reflect upon your own leadership? Explain why you place the ideas you list in a high- or low-priority status.

Chapter 4

Wheat and Chaff
Educational Leadership Uncovered

Wheat and chaff coexist until the very last minute. Chaff, the husk that covers the grain, plays an essential supportive role in the development of wheat. It's discarded during harvest, however, because grain is edible but chaff is not. Threshing describes the process for separating the grain from the husk that once nurtured it.

Separate the wheat from the chaff is a time-honored phrase that recognizes the necessity for leaving behind what was once important to harvest a central idea or understanding. How scholars and practitioners understand educational leadership needs threshing. Like wheat, educational leadership cannot deliver its value if it remains encased.

This chapter is the prose equivalent of threshing. Educational leadership needs to emerge from a husk of scholarship and management. In this chapter, a stipulated concept, *functional educational leadership*, emerges when readers encounter:

- The advent of function of leadership.
- An examination of function and the indeterminate zone of leadership.
- Functional educational leadership and the double helix.
- Harvesting a locus of leadership.

THE ADVENT OF FUNCTION OF LEADERSHIP

Because schools are a *public thing* "to be successful, they must accommodate individual interests and differences in a way that also meets society's common needs and promotes certain shared values and principles" (Knight Abowitz and Stitzlein, 2018, p. 35). The advent of function of leadership in

US public education occurs when all students are valued for their individual lived experience as integral to the common needs and shared principles of US democracy.

Function is activity that is natural to something. A reasonable person could readily identify functions natural to public education—teaching, learning, leading. Similarly, functions natural to leading include being in charge of or commanding something, directing or organizing something, and/or setting things in motion that are aligned with commanding, directing, or organizing.

Apparent clarity about function of leadership, however, does not dissipate the shadows cast by the indeterminate zone (see figure 3.1). Overlapping, conflicting, and/or impractical notions overshadow school leadership and obscure its function. The distortions of scholarship blur the practice of educational leadership. Under these circumstances, school leadership is dimly perceived in a zone characterized by theoretical and practical confusion.

Educational Leadership as an Ecological System

Extricating educational leadership from this functionless zone requires an understanding of schools as a public thing that reflects central ideas of ecological systems theory (Bronfenbrenner, 1979). Bronfenbrenner's contribution to scholarship "is presented as a theory of human development in which everything is seen as interrelated and our knowledge of development is bounded by context, culture, and history" (Darling, 2007, p. 204).

Functional educational leadership borrows from Bronfenbrenner's work in several ways. First, the functions natural to educational leadership are interrelated. Further, development of function of leadership entails agency. Agency is the core of educational leadership: "the central force in development is the active person: shaping environments, evoking responses from them, and reacting to them" (Darling, 2007, p. 204).

In US public education, the active person initiates what Elmore (2005) describes as *alignment*, the "process of moving from an atomized state to a more coherent organizational state" (p. 135). The atomized state of present-day educational leadership is left behind by the intentions of the active person to enact "processes involved in establishing and nurturing a culture of learning and professional behavior" (Goldring, Porter, Murphy, Elliott, and Cravens, 2007, p. 3).

Daly (2009) sheds additional light on function in educational leadership "as comprising a set of complementary competencies that individuals may draw on in providing direction for, and exerting influence in support of, organizational goals" (p. 177). Goldring et al. (2007) call attention to action in leadership which "requires core components created through key processes" (p. 3).

THE DOUBLE HELIX AND FUNCTIONAL EDUCATIONAL LEADERSHIP

These premises of ecological systems theory are evinced in functional educational leadership:

1) Responsive to context,
2) the enactment of dynamic interrelations among functions, and
3) the "active person" choosing, intending, and developing educational environments that all students deserve (Darling, 2007).

The ecology natural to functional educational leadership will be illustrated throughout the remainder of this book in the form of the double helix (see figure 4.1).

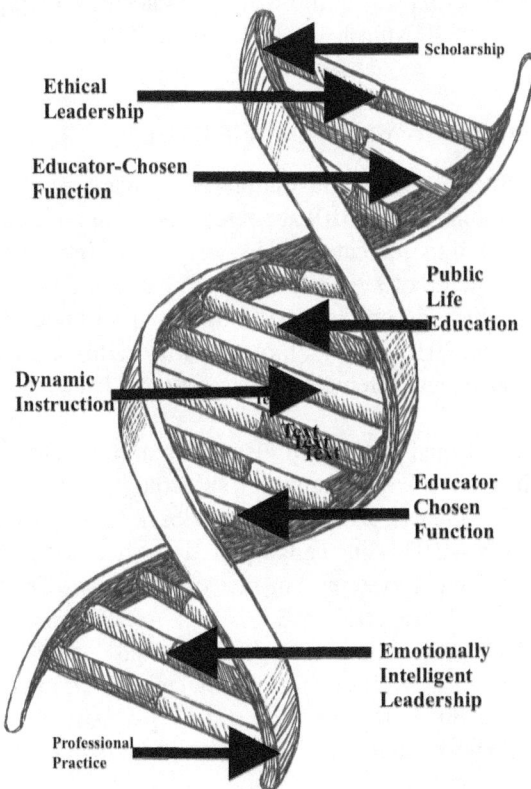

Figure 4.1 *Source*: Purchased from iStock, Stock illustration ID: 490812656, credit: saemilee; adapted by the author.

A Return to Ninth-Grade Biology

A comprehensive view of functional educational leadership mirrors an introductory understanding of DNA in the human body. A return to ninth-grade biology class provides a brief refresher to illustrate the applicability of this metaphor.

The shape of DNA is the double helix. The double helix looks like a ladder (two sides, and rungs that connect the sides) twisted into the shape of corkscrew pasta. Consider professional practice (e.g., the experiences, interactions, and problem solving of day-to-day educating) and scholarship (e.g., research, studies, and the professional practice that applies studies) as the two sides of the double helix shown in figure 4.1.

The rungs of the double helix represent the interconnectivity of functions to access the original power of education, the primary purpose of education, and the moral obligation of public education. The agency and the action of school leadership are facilitated when function within and across the rungs of the double helix is expressed through "variables [that] wrap around each other and mix together" (Murphy et al., 2016, p. 458).

The Theory and Utility of the Double Helix

Utilizing the double helix as an illustration takes advantage of findings articulated by Hallinger and Heck (2010) about leadership and school improvement capacity. These scholars indicate that leadership and improvement capacity "operate as part of a set of systemic relationships. Focusing on one without attending to the others is unlikely to bring about sustained improvement" (Hallinger and Heck, 2010, p. 107). Expanding upon this sense of intentional, holistic, and interrelated interactions, educational leadership becomes an ecology.

Functional educational leadership also takes a cue from ecological systems thinking in that "a key principle of an ecological theory of leadership concerns the importance of diversity and feedback loops" (Wielkiewicz and Stelzner, 2005, p. 334). This cue calls forward the idea that organizations are not *similar to* ecological systems but that organizations *are* these systems (Wielkiewicz and Stelzner, 2005, p. 336).

From this understanding, functional educational leadership emerges as an ecology of functions. Wielkiewicz and Stelzner (2005) indicate that "our definition of leadership is that of an *emergent process*; that is, it emerges from the interactions and actions of individuals within an ecological system" (p. 330).

The vibrant, complex, nature of functional educational leadership, thus, incorporates the scholarly notion of *process* to capture the influence of an individual on a group as a common goal is pursued. "Northouse uses the word 'process' to describe how leaders influence because the word implies an interaction; that is, leaders 'affect and are affected by' those they lead" (Abrahams, 2007, p. 87). The reciprocal nature of influence means that functional educational leadership as *active person* is dialectical and multi-relational.

TOWARD FUNCTIONAL EDUCATIONAL LEADERSHIP: A DEFINITION

Function, the kernel of educational leadership, is wrapped up in the chaff of a multitude of conflicting notions. Too often, the public work of educational leadership lacks clarity. Leadership clarity arises when educators make intentional choices of function necessary and sufficient for the teaching, learning, and futures of all students across lived experience, culture, and context.

To separate the wheat from the chaff in hopes of harvesting clarity for and reliability of educational leadership, a stipulated understanding of *functional educational leadership* will guide the remainder of this discussion: educational leadership is a professional function exercised through interaction between cognition and behavior chosen within the context of a school community to create, sustain, and improve the educational environment that all students deserve.

Santamaria and Santamaria (2015) give voice to reliability sought via this sense of functional educational leadership as "an interdisciplinary, dynamic, multidimensional process that is context embedded and specific to people, places, and time" (p. 23).

The Double Helix: Shaping Educational Leadership

The importance of the double helix as a metaphor lies in its applicability. Functional educational leadership, like DNA, is always building and rebuilding, communicating and initiating, so that agency for the educational environments that all US public school students deserve is omnipresent. Leadership in this way is initiating, responsive, and self-correcting.

The significance of the double helix is that this design incorporates the multiple seamless connections among ideas, information, skills, experience, data, and behaviors within context made manifest by functional educational leadership. The rungs in this double helix are the source of agency throughout functional educational leadership.

HARVESTING EDUCATIONAL LEADERSHIP

Although our nation's farming origins no longer dominate America's thinking, agricultural metaphors can reorient present-day thinking about educational leadership. The statement (often spoken by a grateful farm owner during a bountiful family meal), "there is enough food to feed the threshers," extends the central theme of this chapter.

Implied by this statement is that the hard work done by the relatively small group who thresh the grain assures the sustenance and livelihood of many others. The work of separating grain from chaff fulfilled the purpose and delivered the benefits of farming. Chaff-free educational leadership, in the same way, can provide an ample harvest of educational environments in which all students are nourished. A harvest of leadership that benefits everyone.

Can Educational Leadership Function Reliably?

Public educators are quick to proclaim that their professional intention is to benefit all students. But how educational leadership is to harvest this intention reliably is largely unknown. As scholars indicate, "leadership is arguably one of the most observed, yet least understood phenomena on earth" (Amanchukwu, Stanley, and Ololube, 2015, p. 6).

Urick and Bowers (2014) acknowledge the dysfunctional effects of historic and present-day thinking about educational leadership and recommend that future research into the influence of principals "focus on measuring their leadership using a set of core behaviors . . . or multiple leadership styles in order to capture a complete range of leadership tasks rather than limiting principal behavior to individual leadership styles" (Urick and Bowers, 2014, p. 121).

Most of the time, however, scholars and practitioners fail to put choice and intention in the hands of educators. Indicating that there are many prepackaged forms of leadership, however, is not the same as constituting the active person in leadership as central to a developing, emerging, interconnected, and intentional process.

The present-day tendency to investigate leadership by measuring how often different styles or theories of leadership behavior occur is a fruitless enterprise. A tally of leadership "acts" fails to evaluate how well these behaviors, choices, and intentions generate the purpose, mission, and outcomes that all students deserve from public education.

This failure prompts a difficult question: Why do scholarly and practical notions about the nature of educational leadership conflict, collide, and mislead to the point that educators do not function reliably to deliver the promises of US public education? Reliable school leadership to ensure that all students fulfill their potential is not, yet, within the locus of leadership of twenty-first-century public education.

Learning Is Leadership Fuel

Within this transformed understanding of educational leadership lies what a school leader knows and what a school leader continues to learn. Scholarship and research that a leader incorporates into his/her agency are choices that relate to context and that fuel agency. Agency is nurtured when a leader groups or organizes her/his prior learning and ongoing scholarship for day-to-day access as suggested in these representative research summaries:

- *Overarching theories of leadership:*
  - "Classical management and role-theory"
  - "Transactional leadership theory"
  - "Transformational leadership theory"
  - "Horizontal or collaborative leadership theory"
  - Ethical and critical leadership theory" (Van Wart, 2013, p. 553).
- *Four classifications of leadership:*
  - "Building vision and setting direction"
  - "Understanding and developing people"
  - The AERA Task Force that advanced this as a component of successful leadership indicated it is comprised of "practices that 'significantly and positively influence the motivation and capacities of their colleagues' (Leithwood and Riehl, 2003, p. 19)" (Daly, 2009, p. 178).
- *"Redesigning the organization"*
  - The AERA Task Force that brought this component of successful school leadership forward described it "as the ability of leaders to 'develop their schools as effective organizations that support and sustain the performance of teachers as well as students (Leithwood and Riehl, 2003, p. 20)'" (Daly, 2009, p. 178).
- managing the learning program (Klar and Brewer, 2013).*

  *[Authors' note: Leithwood, Harris, and Hopkins (2008) make seven claims about successful school leadership and one of them is that "almost all successful leaders draw on the same repertoire of basic leadership practices" (p. 29). These scholars organize these basic practices into the four categories listed above. Although prepackaged clusters of leadership practices name behaviors relevant to leadership, they illustrate the limitations fostered by the piece-by-piece approach to educational leadership.]

- *Three dimensions of instructional leadership*
  - "Defining the School's Mission,

- Managing the Instructional Program, and
- Promoting a Positive School Learning Climate (Hallinger, 2001; Hallinger and Murphy, 1985a)" (Hallinger, 2005, p. 4).
• *Hierarchical taxonomy of meta-categories of leadership behaviors*
  - Task-oriented
  - Relations-oriented
  - Change-oriented
  - External (Yukl, 2012, p. 68).

The complexities inherent in public education, a history of overlapping research and disjointed practice, and the entanglements created by ideology encase present-day educational leadership. Discarding this husk is the task facing educators if a reimagined educational leadership is to emerge. Separating the chaff that surrounds present-day notions of school leadership harvests function to nurture a transformation of educational leadership.

Functional educational leadership (portrayed as a double helix) presents the opportunity to reimagine leadership throughout America's public schools. To facilitate enactment of the leadership that all students deserve for the remainder of the twenty-first century, four examples of functions—dynamic instruction; ethical leadership; emotionally intelligent leadership; public life education—will be discussed in the next chapters.

LOOKING AT THIS CHAPTER IN THE REARVIEW MIRROR

School leaders work hard. The public work of educators necessitates decision-making and intentionality so that the kernel of leading sustains the school community, the original power of education, and dynamic instruction. To ensure that educational leadership in practice reaps the benefits of scholarship and, at the same time, is not covered up by the multiple conflicting notions that restrict leading, functional educational leadership is introduced in this chapter.

Future chapters in this discussion will explore the agency, the challenges, and the benefits that arise from functional educational leadership. This will be an exploration galvanized to a central concept: educational leadership is a professional function exercised through interaction between cognition and behavior chosen within context to create, sustain, and improve educational environments that all students deserve.

At this point, readers can harvest their own impressions about leadership function by crafting responses to these questions:

- Paraphrase how functional educational leadership is described in this chapter; how does this compare or contrast with educational leadership as you perceive it?
- Is it possible for the multiple conflicting perspectives generated by scholarship to inform functional educational leadership but be separate from it in practice? Explain your thinking.
- Why do the many notions about the nature of educational leadership fail to establish substantive academic proficiency for all students?
- What needs to be accomplished in your school or school district and in your professional practice to enact functional educational leadership?

Chapter 5

Our Students Deserve—Dynamic Instruction

All students in US public schools deserve educational environments suffused with high-quality instruction. This level of instruction is the professional practice of educators created by "highly complex sets of skills, intellectual functioning and knowledge that are not easily acquired and not widely held" (Ingersoll and Collins, 2017, p. 90).

Students engage with knowledge, creativity, complex thinking skills, and emotion when educators create and deliver instruction with a profound influence on meaning-making. Teachers are not the only professional educators responsible for this positive impact; research indicates that school leaders have an indirect effect on students' academic proficiency (Waters and Marzano, 2007).

The level of day-to-day instruction that engages all students with learning necessary for personal success and for success as adults in American democracy will be referred to as *dynamic instruction* throughout the remainder of this discussion.

Dynamic instruction is a rung in the double helix of functional educational leadership. Dynamic instruction is expressed in *leadership of instruction* and *leadership for instruction*. At the core of this chapter lies the premise that dynamic instruction is function chosen and implemented by teachers and designated school leaders (e.g., team leaders, department chairs, principals, superintendents). Readers will engage with a dialogue that explores:

- Agency and action of functional educational leadership;
- Instructional leadership: the sound of silence;
- "The default culture of public schools" (Elmore, 2005, p. 134);
- Pivoting to functional educational leadership;
- The nature of dynamic instruction; and
- The pedagogies of dynamic instruction.

THE CASE FOR DYNAMIC INSTRUCTION AS FUNCTION

A function is an activity natural to something. Throughout US public education, professional educators aspire to enact the activities natural to their assigned roles. Common sense would dictate that innumerable functions—including instruction—are natural activities of public education. But a paradox is alive and well in present-day public education. Although instruction is a function of leadership essential for the academic success of US students, an absence of agency and action ensures that *instructional leadership* is little more than a popular buzzword.

Why Leadership and Instruction Disconnect

Early in this century, Hallinger (2005) observed "there is little evidence to support the view that on a broad scale at either the elementary or secondary school level principals have become more engaged in hands-on directed supervision of teaching and learning in classrooms" (p. 10). More than a decade after this accounting, Murphy et al. (2016) reached the strikingly similar conclusion "that for all the evidence and recognition of importance, learning-focused leadership remains a small domain of action for leaders at the school levels" (p. 460).

An explanation for this incongruity is identified by studies that found that "a lack of clear knowledge about how student learning and other outcomes are produced works against emphasis on instructional management behavior in the principalship" (Murphy et al., 2016, p. 464).

Exceptions to this prevalent state of affairs do exist. One of the authors served as principal of an elementary school in an urban district where school leaders were charged with spending 70 percent of their weekly schedule with activities directly tied to instruction. Rethinking the school day, principals and assistant principals adopted a walk-through model to ensure time in every teacher's classroom at least four times a week. The expectation that all students experienced significant direct instruction coupled with this model led to increased student engagement in learning and fewer classroom behavior issues.

The expectation that instruction is an activity natural to education and educational leadership is, nevertheless, an unusually fraught proposition. Murphy et al. (2016) give this state of affairs historical context when they observe that "since instructional management was pushed onto the school administrator stage some 35 years ago with the start of the school effectiveness movement, time devoted to instructional work has changed very little" (p. 455).

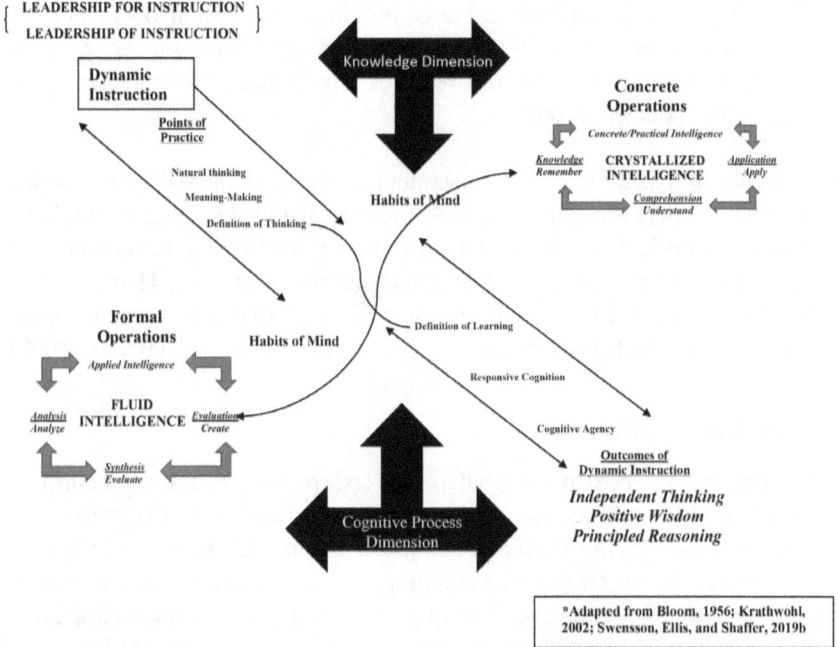

Figure 5.1 Instructional Function. *Source*: Adapted from Bloom, B. (Ed.) (1956). *Taxonomy of Educational Objectives: The Classification of Educational Goals*. New York: Longmans Green; Krathwohl, D. R. (2002). "A Revision of Bloom's Taxonomy: An overview." *Theory Into Practice* (41)4, 212–218. Retrieved from https://www.depauw.edu/files/resources/krathwohl; Swensson, J., Ellis, J., and Shaffer, M. (2019b). *An Educator's GPS: Fending Off the Free Market of Schooling for America's Students*. London: Rowman & Littlefield.

Leadership *of Instruction* and Leadership *for Instruction*

As illustrated in figure 5.1, reimagining *dynamic instruction* as a function of educational leadership originates in the relationship between leadership *for instruction* and leadership *of instruction*. This relationship exists because all US public educators begin their careers as teachers.

Leadership *of Instruction*

Teachers exercise leadership *of instruction*. Leadership of instruction has a direct effect on learning. Two research-based fundamentals convey the value of this agency and action:

- "Instruction and classroom environments have the greatest impact on student learning" (Seashore Louis, Dretzke, and Wahlstrom, 2010, p. 316).

- "Teaching is not just a technical or cognitive practice but also an emotional one (Hargreaves, 1998). Teaching expresses teachers' own feelings, and affects the feelings of others. It requires 'emotional understanding' (Denzin, 1984)" (Beatty, 2000).

Leadership *of instruction* is the enactment of the fundamental understanding that "who teachers are and the values, knowledge and skills that they bring to teaching are critical to school and student success. Equally important, what they do matters a good deal (Darling-Hammond and Post; Hattie, 2009)" (Murphy et al., 2016, p. 456). Leadership *of instruction* recognizes and accounts for the fact that "teaching is an emotional practice" (Beatty, 2000).

Leadership *for Instruction*

Educators who serve in designated leadership roles enact leadership *for instruction*. The indirect effect of leadership *for instruction* is represented in activities like giving feedback about lessons; modeling dynamic instructional strategies; creating and sustaining viable educational environments; engaging with all colleagues about quality teaching behaviors; and/or establishing a positive climate for teaching, learning, and the moral obligation of public education (Murphy et al., 2016, pp. 456–457; Swensson and Shaffer, 2020).

Hallinger and Heck (2010) confirm that a successful public school leader is responsible for the educational environment that undergirds high-quality teaching and learning (p. 97). Marzano, Waters, and McNulty (2005) speak to the impact of school leaders when they note "a highly effective school leader can have a dramatic influence on the overall academic achievement of students" (p. 10). Leadership *for instruction* is the professional intention to manifest:

- *An Eye on the Prize:* The prize, in the case of dynamic instruction, is student engagement with the original power of education in the intersection of *how to think* and the moral obligation of public education. Accessing the original power of education is the primary objective of both leadership *of instruction* and leadership *for instruction*. Sustaining an eye on the prize allows educators to evolve dynamic instruction and to align homegrown assessments with the habits of mind that students experience during instruction. Reliable school leadership is fostered when educators do not take their eyes off the prize.
- *Active Learning:* If learning in public education was ever about only memorizing facts, those days are gone. The premise behind dynamic instruction is that all learning is more effective when students are actively

engaged in applying thinking skills or habits of mind (Swensson and Shaffer, 2020). Active learning, then, is about students applying habits of mind to investigate, resolve, wonder about, and/or consider problems, dilemmas, unknowns, and paradoxes.
- *A Loop:* In computing, a loop is a sequence of instructions in a program repeated during or until some sought-after condition is satisfied. Borrowing from this understanding, active learning incorporates habits of mind/thinking skills looped by dynamic instruction throughout a school year and interconnected with learning from other classrooms and/or from previous school years. Active learning lessons "loop" these thinking skills back and forth between prior knowledge and newly taught knowledge, skills, processes, concepts, and emotions. Dynamic instruction is both direct and indirect in the sense that educators introduce and demonstrate habits of mind while guiding instruction back to previously encountered constructs while students are engaged with active, authentic learning: solving a problem, completing a welding assignment, experiencing a classroom simulation, undertaking a lab experiment, creating an artistic project, or expressing a musical interpretation.

The impact of dynamic instruction as a function of educational leadership is derived from what will be referred to during this discussion as *the original power of education.*

The Original Power of Education

The original power of education is expressed in a "pedagogical exchange as a form of value creation rather than knowledge transmission" (McWilliam, 2008, p. 266). The original power of education occurs in the dialectic between teaching and learning. "This exchange occurs during classroom construction of the intersection of *how to think* and the moral obligation of public education" (Swensson and Shaffer, 2020, p. 67). The value creation resulting from the dialectic between teaching and learning is the original power of education.

In this exchange, *teaching* is the power to *lead-out* student intelligences with knowledge, cognitive process, and/or skills beyond their personal assets. *Learning* is the power for meaning-making that begins for every person in natural thinking, and multiple capacities including lived experience (Swensson and Shaffer, 2020).

Educational leadership has a responsibility to ensure that the original power of education is the agency of *leading-out* in the ecology of a school or school district. Figure 5.2 illustrates the essential elements of the original

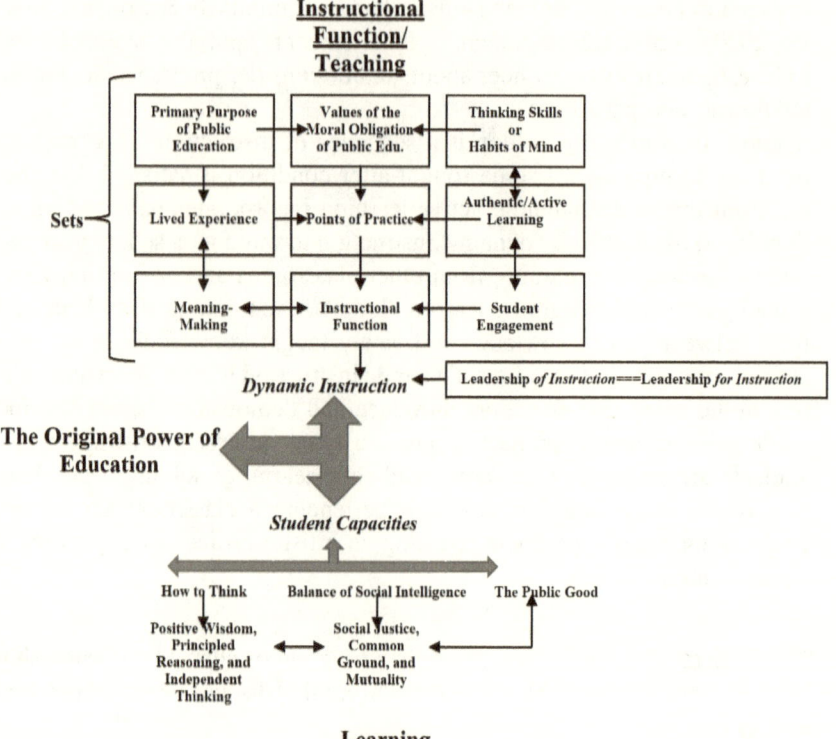

Figure 5.2   The Original Power of Education. *Source:* Author created.

power of education and the dialectic between teaching and learning that dynamic instruction ought to create.

The original power of education supplies its own feedback. For instance, leadership *of instruction* generates feedback "as teachers develop their capacity to use 'formative,' internally-generated data to refine and improve their practice, [and] they often produce 'significant and often substantial learning gains' (Black and William, 1998, p. 3)" (Cohen-Vogel and Harrison, 2013, p. 126).

IF INSTRUCTIONAL LEADERSHIP FELL IN A CLASSROOM, WOULD IT MAKE A SOUND?

Instructional leadership is a well-known phrase and an abundantly researched concept. But notoriety is one thing and day-to-day practice is another. It turns out that the mega-decibel conversation about instructional leadership generates barely a whisper during day-to-day teaching and learning. The imperative for reimagining educational leadership to enact function is abundantly clear because when instructional leadership falls in classrooms across America, the sound of silence is the usual result.

The "why" used to justify the frenzy over instructional leadership is abundantly simple: it's supposed to influence student achievement positively. To realize this outcome, school leaders are "expected to understand the tenets of quality instruction, as well as have sufficient knowledge of the curriculum to know that appropriate content is being delivered to all students (Marzano et al., 2005)" (Seashore Louis, Dretzke, and Wahlstrom, 2010, p. 317).

Why, then, does school leadership have such a limited effect on the academic outcomes that are supposed to emerge when instructional leadership engages with teaching (Leithwood, Harris, and Hopkins, 2008)?

Research indicates that school leaders "continue to be unsuccessful at meeting the academic standards set by the state and federal accountability models (Dillon, 2010; Styron and Styron, 2011)" (Quin et al., 2015, pp. 71–72). The weak impact of instructional leadership is highlighted in research findings that show that "it is debatable if a significant difference exists in the leadership practices of principals in high performing and low performing schools" (Quin et al., 2015, p. 73).

The Interminable Cacophony of Standardized Testing

Any impact that instructional leadership could have on academic proficiency is drowned out by "the introduction of performance-based accountability— policies that evaluate, reward, and sanction schools on the basis of measured performance" (Elmore, 2005, p. 134). Inquiry into performance-based accountability "suggests that school principals are changing how they define their responsibilities to focus more on leading and managing instruction, especially in tested subjects" (Spillane, Parise, and Zoltners Sherer, 2011, p. 590).

It turns out that the ballyhooed impact of instructional leadership is absent so often from the practice of school leaders that it should be considered truant. Standardized testing, by comparison, has perfect attendance. This reversal does not enhance student thinking, behavior, or creativity. School leaders manage by riveting instruction to the requirements of standardized testing.

Snared in the trap of standardized testing, instructional leadership is reduced "to narrowing the school curriculum for mathematics and language arts to skills that were tested and to marginalizing other school subjects" (Spillane, Parise, and Zoltners Sherer, 2011, p. 614). Practitioners and scholars alike call the resulting pseudo-instruction *test-prep*.

Present-day leadership for instruction is backward. Instead of accessing the original power of education to transform the capabilities of all students, instructional leadership is transformed by accountability. Management further reinforces tendencies for *transforming backward* amidst what has been described as the default culture in public education.

MAROONED ON THE ISLAND OF DEFAULT CULTURE

Surrounded by a sea of expectations and restrictions associated with standardized testing, and beholden to the ideology of free market schooling, leadership in US public education is marooned on *the island of default culture* (Elmore, 2005). Policy and statute aid and abet this culture by interposing free market theory between school leadership and instruction as if efficiency ought to be the primary goal of public education.

Compelled to ensure that teaching and learning fulfill the expectations of standardized testing, educators are stranded in a default culture "characterized by the atomization or fragmentation of teaching, the buffering of instructional practice from external influence, and the belief that teaching is primarily an 'art' that is not susceptible to systematic and replicable knowledge" (Elmore, 2005, p. 134).

Transforming Backward in the Default Culture

Cut off from the original power of education and from the dynamic instruction that delivers this power, educators lose sight of the enduring impact of instruction on student learning: "instruction trumps programs, student grouping patterns, choice arrangements, and all other school factors (Supovitz and Turner, 2000; Wahlstrom and Louis, 2008)" (Murphy et al., 2016, p. 456).

The default culture short-circuits power. Function of educational leadership is stranded by this investment in standardized test data, knee-jerk pedagogy, test-prep, and a narrowed curriculum. Moreover, immersion in this culture can introduce, or reinforce, educators' negative perceptions of the capacities of students for learning. When the default culture fails to create, or improve, academic proficiency, educators "tend to attribute the lack of success to the characteristics of the students" (Elmore, 2005, p. 139).

When adults blame students, they engage with the bigotry of deficit-thinking and permit stereotype threat nurtured within the exclusionary mentality fostered by free market theory (Swensson and Shaffer, 2020). Students become grist for the mill of an ideological blame game that separates them from the original power of public education, dynamic instruction, and the moral obligation of public education. Too often, transforming backward is the result of a school culture destabilized by free market theory.

FUNCTIONAL EDUCATIONAL LEADERSHIP: AGENCY AND ACTION

Agency, amidst all its manifestations (Matusov, von Duyke, and Kayumova, 2016), gives voice to the intentionality necessary for a school leader to enact function:

- *Instrumental.* "Instrumental agency focuses on human mastery; having the capacities to do and accomplish something successfully" (Matusov, von Duyke, and Kayumova, 2016, p. 426). Instrumental agency is "a tool to do something socially valuable, and predefined in advance" (Matusov, von Duyke, and Kayumova, 2016, p. 426).
- *Relational.* Relational agency is "based on a fluid and open-ended notion" of Vygotsky's zone of proximal development (Matusov, von Duyke, and Kayumova, 2016, p. 426). Vygotsky's notion "refers to functions that have not yet matured but are in the process of maturation" (Sternberg and Grigorenko, 2004, p. 279). Relational agency facilitates the evolution of leadership and function.
- *Both/and.* Agency of functional educational leadership is *both/and* which is represented in the conjunction of single-loop learning and double-loop learning. "Single-loop learning is learning 'that does not question the fundamental goals, design and activities of [the] organization' whereas in double-loop learning 'participants would be able to ask questions about changing fundamental aspects of the organization'" (Park, Hironaka, Carver, and Nordstrom, 2013).

Agency, further, entails an educator's lived experience, culture, ethnicity, race, gender orientation, language, and professional training. These aspects of life and learning enrich agency with the "ability to use one's talents effectively, to learn from both good and bad experiences, to thoroughly understand one's current situation, and to establish a sense of character and competence" (Van Wart, 2013, p. 553).

Action for Functional Educational Leadership

Action is the direction in which agency takes function to ensure that all students experience learning environments that they deserve. Leithwood, Harris, and Hopkins (2008) indicate the effect of action in their finding that a school leader's "strongest direct contribution to altered classroom practices was teachers' beliefs about their capacity to implement [instructional] strategies" (p. 33).

The effect of action is demonstrated by findings "that teachers may, in their own work, be bridging the scholarly debates between constructivist and direct instruction by developing strategies that are designed to incorporate elements of both" (Fisher and Frey, 2008; Seashore Louis, Dretzke, and Wahlstrom, 2010, p. 322).

For learners engaged by principled reasoning, social justice, positive liberty, and independent thinking that empower a future of citizenship participation in US democracy, "*action* is giving birth to new ideas and meanings through speech and 'political action in concert among equals' (Honig, 1988, p. 41)" (Knight Abowitz, 2018, p. 8).

DYNAMIC INSTRUCTION IN A LEADER'S DAY

Dynamic instruction—an admixture of an educator's science, art, pedagogy, lived experience, information, care, cognitive process, creativity, intellect, data, and emotion—*leads-out* the capacities of all students. Dynamic instruction engages students in educational environments where inquiry, project-based simulations, active learning, and other authentic learning opportunities construct an intersection between how to think and the values of the moral obligation of public education.

Leadership *of instruction* or leadership *for instruction* represent agency and action of educators undeterred by obstacles to function. Dynamic instruction in a leader's day, thus, can include engaging with colleagues in decision-making about instructional methods; providing detailed feedback to colleagues from frequent classroom visits; sharing and researching best practices to grow the capacities of both colleagues and students; and devoting time to the persistent pursuit of teaching that engages all students fully (Murphy et al., 2016, p. 457).

Leadership that prepares students as national citizens in a global society creates educational environments where dynamic instruction generates "critical thinking, communication, collaboration, and creativity" (Minkos et al., 2017, p. 1263).

Enacting dynamic instruction incorporates coaching—one action of leadership *for instruction*—to sustain leadership *of instruction* anchored by habits of mind and the values of the moral obligation of public education. Intertwined with emotional intelligence, dynamic instruction functions to establish "a school culture that allows students to feel comfortable sharing their ideas, beliefs, values, and opinions [and this] is fundamental to student success (Fraise and Brooks, 2015)" (Minkos et al., 2017, p. 1262).

Dynamic instruction does not marginalize or deny; learning cannot occur if these threats loom over students. As a function, dynamic instruction interacts throughout the double helix so that each student learns to be guided by her/his own reasoning in support of the mutuality of individual and public benefits vouchsafed by US democracy (Fraser-Burgess, 2012; Swensson and Shaffer, 2020).

The Pedagogies of Dynamic Instruction

Agency and action undergird the pedagogies of dynamic instruction. Murphy et al. (2016) detail the pedagogical impact of leadership *for instruction*: "A school's leadership is likely to have more positive impacts on student achievement and well-being if it is able to focus on the quality of learning, teaching, and teacher learning" (pp. 456–458).

Complex and Soundly Structured Pedagogy

Dynamic instruction is an investment in what Kurth-Schai (2014) refers to as *complex pedagogy*. Complex pedagogy evolves from collaboration among leaders "to prepare the environment and facilitate the relationships necessary to support diverse learners as they experience social inquiry, discover shared purpose, and translate collective goals into principled action" (Kurth-Schai, 2014, p. 432).

Complex pedagogy incorporates what Schmoker (2019) describes as *soundly structured instruction* which, in part, includes "a clear statement of what will be learned, why it's worth learning, and how it will be assessed" (p. 28). The pedagogies shared during leadership *of instruction* are those during which "successful teachers are not simply charismatic, persuasive and expert presenters; rather, they create powerful cognitive and social tasks to their students and teach the students how to make productive use of them" (Hopkins, 2003, p. 61).

Dynamic instruction demonstrates the complex pedagogy chosen and implemented when leadership *of instruction* and leadership *for instruction* converge. "When instructional leadership is shared among the teachers *and* with the principal, the influence of the combined efforts on the quality of pedagogy is significant" (Wahlstrom and Seashore Louis, 2008, p. 483).

Complex Pedagogy and All Students

Dynamic instruction generates environments in which "improvement of *student academic outcomes* (Bamburg and Andrews, 1990; Glasman, 1984; Goldring and Pasternak, 1994; Hallinger and Murphy, 1986; Heck et al., 1990; Leithwood, Begley and Cousins, 1990; Leitner, 1994; O'Day, 1983)" (emphasis original) (Hallinger, 2005, p. 4) is the primary purpose of public education.

Research suggests the value of dynamic instruction when leadership intentions converge. The academic success of students is more likely in schools where "teachers created instruction in which students were more involved in conversation and activity related to lesson objectives and were less likely to be expected to sit quietly and listen" (Johnson Jr. and Willis, 2013, p. 448).

Dynamic instruction incorporates culturally responsive pedagogy which "'validates, facilitates, liberates, and empowers ethnically diverse students by simultaneously cultivating their cultural integrity, individual abilities, and academic success' (p. 46)" (Johnson Jr. and Willis, 2013, p. 437). Student learning is enhanced when "communication, curricula, and instruction are shaped in ways that acknowledge, honor, and reflect their language, heritage, prior knowledge, and learning styles" (Johnson Jr. and Willis, 2013, p. 443).

CAN EDUCATIONAL LEADERSHIP PIVOT?

Faced with the debilitating impact of default culture, the anemic effect of instructional leadership, and the strictures imposed by standardized testing, can present-day school leadership pivot to enact dynamic instruction? Three opportunities to pivot are available to present-day educational leadership:

Pivot Opportunity #1

To pivot, educators must, first, take a cue from Bandura's (1983) articulation of *self-efficacy*, the belief that one's actions will make a difference. Believing that actions make a difference inspires intentionality, facilitates sensitivity, and launches the agency of function. Goldring and Greenfield (2002) confirm, for instance, that "teachers' practices are driven largely by their beliefs about what works" (p. 7).

But the impediments in default culture have a debilitating effect on self-efficacy. When, as is presently the case in this age of accountability (Swensson, Ellis, and Shaffer, 2019b), educational practice is largely function-less, the results of teaching and learning promote the belief that if public education makes a difference, the difference is likely to be at the low end of a continuum of possible results. Can school leaders shift to demonstrating to colleagues, parents/caregivers, and citizens that dynamic instruction makes a difference for all students?

Pivot Opportunity #2

Next, educators can pivot by enacting dynamic instruction to make a difference in the lives of their students. The difference that all public educators want to make as professionals entails the dedication to *lead-out* the thinking and behaviors of all students (Swensson, Ellis, and Shaffer, 2019a). Can the self-efficacy of educators manifest itself in function which, in turn, becomes the pivot to nurturing the self-efficacy of students engaged with the original power of education?

In practical terms, leadership *for instruction* and leadership *of instruction* intertwine to design and implement "sets" of instructional function that interrelate to build the original power of education in the educational environments of schools and school districts as shown in figure 5.2. The sets or building blocks of the original power of education contribute to the agency of dynamic instruction and put students in position to engage cognitively, behaviorally, and emotionally in the intersection of primary purpose and the moral obligation of public education.

Pivot Opportunity #3

Finally, educators can pivot when their efforts infuse each practitioner's paradigm about the *leadership differential* in US public education. Organizations, including public education, designate various roles or positions in the organization to perform specific leadership tasks and undertake different leadership behaviors.

This differentiation of leadership assignments and tasks throughout public education, however, does not mean that the function of dynamic instruction is the exclusive province of one designated position or another. The activities associated with this function emerge from self-efficacy, the agency and action of individual educators, and the collaboration between educators.

Nuancing the Leadership Differential

Leadership is the intentional interconnectivities between functions manifest in agency and action. Some functional educational leadership is associated with, or required by, a designated role in an organization. Under these circumstances, the functions of educational leadership are stipulated for a position in an organization to enact activities that guide, direct, inspire, and/or motivate other individuals or groups to carry out differentiated roles and to enact functions.

Dynamic instruction is not exclusive to a designated role or position in a school or school district. As Wahlstrom and Seashore Louis (2008) observe, "when the power differential between principals and teachers is lessened, instruction is positively affected" (p. 483).

Dynamic instruction puts educators in position to take responsibility for "the instructional program and creating a productive culture, or 'school as academic place and productive community'" (Murphy et al., 2016, p. 459). Across the rungs of the double helix, educators enact process—"organizational functioning processes, human relations processes, and inspirational processes" (Murphy et al., 2016, p. 459)—to craft dynamic instruction.

DYNAMIC INSTRUCTION: A RUNG THAT STUDENTS DESERVE

Dynamic instruction—agency and action for educational environments where the intersection between *how to think* and the moral obligation of public education challenges and develops the capacities of all students—is rare in the era of standardized assessment and accountability. "'Our fear of uncertainty drives us to teach our students to live in intellectual, cultural, and political silos that leave no room for ambiguity, relationality, or engagement' (Cortez and Delpit, 2010, 93–96)" (Kurth-Schai, 2014, p. 432).

Under the present circumstances that afflict US public education, both *leadership of* and *leadership for* instruction have been ignored and an instructional vacuum exists instead. This vacuum, often labeled as "reform" for public education, is a place where "data has been used to provide a causal relationship between input (classroom activities) and outputs (test scores)" (Rice, 2017, p. 58).

Instead of linear expectations about inputs and outputs posing as education, dynamic instruction embraces expectations for student engagement (cognitive, emotional, and behavioral) with what scholars have termed *evolutionary learning* (Kurth-Schai, 2014, p. 434).

In this case, function is enacted for evolutionary learning acquired from the original power of education. This transformational outcome is fostered because "people and institutions learn when they focus their attention on concrete problems that link meaning tightly to action" (Kurth-Schai, 2014, p. 434). Evolving, growing, reflecting, and problem-solving, functional educational leadership allows all students to attain personal and civic agency for action.

The worth of dynamic instruction lies in this agency. Studies demonstrate, for example, that students who experience social and emotional learning in classrooms earn significantly higher grades than students in educational environments where there is no focus on habits of mind or the behaviors of social and emotional learning (Hoffman, Ivcevic, and Brackett, 2018).

Kurth-Schai (2014) identifies how dynamic instruction suffuses the double helix of functional educational leadership with agency for complex pedagogies necessary and sufficient for:

- "ensuring free and full participation of all participants, with special attention devoted to the deliberative challenges posed for historically disadvantaged populations,"
- "integrating varied dimensions of human experience and understanding (intellectual, emotional, intuitive, aesthetic, sensory)," and
- "supporting sustained engagement in principled and effective social action" (p. 436).

The pedagogies of dynamic instruction facilitate a teacher's promotion of "student learning by being active in planning and organising his or her teaching, explaining to students what they are to learn, arranging occasions for guided practice, monitoring progress, providing feedback, and otherwise helping students understand and accomplish work" (Hopkins, 2003, p. 62). America's students deserve everything that dynamic instruction can give them.

LOOKING AT THIS CHAPTER IN THE REARVIEW MIRROR

Creating the conditions that can restore instruction to the purview of leadership in schools means, first, ending the lip service given to instructional leadership as if it is present in, and as if it is separate from, leadership *per se*. "Research into administrative practice in schools has found an unmistakable pattern of practice whereby principals tended to avoid the instructional role even in the face of contrary normative expectations (e.g., Cuban, 1988; Wolcott, 1973)" (Hallinger, 2005, p. 11).

This chapter explores the counterproductive influence of "instructional methods [that] are stringently standardized to ensure quality control and ease of replication. Implementation processes are also carefully controlled, and most often reliant upon authoritative, often charismatic, leadership" (Kurth-Schai, 2014, p. 425).

Intentions that readers bring to leadership, function, dynamic instruction, and educational environments that all students deserve can be examined by responding to these questions:

- Hallinger (2005) recalls a quotation: "Educational administration is a bus schedule with footnotes by Kierkegaard" (p. 12). And Hallinger follows

Kierkegaard's comment with a question: Does this quotation describe leadership in US public education accurately? Explain your answer to this question in detail.
- Summarize the current state of the relationship between instruction and leadership shared in this chapter. Describe how well or how poorly this depiction aligns with this same relationship in your school district.
- Put into your own words the value of agency and action for educators and give examples of both and their impact from your own professional experiences.
- Paraphrase the practical implications of the ideas about functional educational leadership presented in this chapter when they are applied to the school setting where you are employed.

Chapter 6

Our Students Deserve— Ethical Leadership

Speaking about *ethical leadership* or the *ethics of leadership* ought to be as redundant as speaking about an "ATM machine." ATM, after all, is the acronym for Automatic Teller Machine. By the same token, leadership already entails, or ought to entail, *ethics*. Scholars observe that "what students of educational administration call practice is chiefly an ethical undertaking, that is, a matter of the reflective appraisal of the values served by various decision options" (Greenfield, 2004, p. 185).

Unfortunately, the decision-making, choices, and behaviors of school leaders do not always entail ethics. This chapter invites readers to consider what it takes to ensure that speaking about ethical leadership *is* unnecessary. *Being ethical* and the direct effects of ethics in leadership will be explored in this chapter through:

- a discussion about the rationale for ethics in school leadership;
- an examination of the difference between using ethics and *being* ethical;
- identification of the building blocks of ethics;
- dialogue about the baseline of and the challenges for ethics in school leadership;
- a view of the upside-down history of ethics in American education; and
- an understanding of the moral obligation of US public education.

THE RATIONALE FOR ETHICS IN LEADERSHIP

Ultimately, leadership is about choosing. The expression of ethics in leadership depends on how leaders choose and the extent to which the choices are linked to values, morals, and virtue. "Ethics is concerned with the kinds of values and morals an individual or society finds desirable or appropriate. Furthermore, ethics is concerned with the virtuousness of individuals and their motives" (Northouse, 2007, p. 342).

Leaders must confront and evaluate persistently their own sense of virtue and how this ethical guide aligns with what is appropriate, reasonable, fair, and just. For US public educators, alignment of leadership ought to be measured by "'the method of democracy, of a positive toleration which amounts to sympathetic regard for the intelligence and personality of others, even if they hold views opposed to ours' (Dewey, 1932, p. 329)" (Kurth-Schai, 2014, p. 429).

Ethical choices that sustain the tenets of US democracy and the values of the moral obligation of public education reflect the integrity of leadership. Two fundamental questions allow school leaders to judge the extent to which their choices align with the method of democracy and the degree to which integrity guides their behavior:

(1) Does the leader "treat people as ends in themselves" (Greenfield, 2004, p. 180), and (2) does the leader see all human beings as resourceful instead of viewing human beings as resources that can be manipulated?

Using Ethics Is Not the Same as *Being* Ethical

At first glance, the connections between ethics and school leadership are straightforward: "It is incumbent upon school leaders to make ethical decisions that truly reflect the needs of students and not their own adult self-interest" (Stefkovich and Begley, 2007, p. 215). Through reflection* upon the two questions suggested above by Greenfield (2004), educational leaders ought to be able to avoid adult-centric decisions and behaviors with ease.

[*Authors' note: Experience has taught us that reflection is an invaluable leadership activity. Reflecting about information, interactions, dilemmas, goals, decisions, and possibilities, leaders generate resources required for being ethical. We cannot overemphasize the worth of reflection. Among the demands that all leaders make of themselves, persistent reflection must be given top priority.]

Being ethical is easier said than done because school leaders must have "the ability to distinguish the difference between using ethics and being ethical" (Stefkovich and Begley, 2007, p. 211). The ability to differentiate between *being* ethical and using ethics is critical for educational leaders because it is possible to use ethics to choose and justify unethical decisions and/or immoral actions.

For instance, as Stefkovich and Begley (2007) point out, prohibiting hats in school to ensure a focus on academics while preventing gang confrontations is an example of *being* ethical. But if the underlying objective of such a prohibition is to ban the headgear of certain religions, ethics are used to impose cultural and religious discrimination.

A second glance at the ease of *being* ethical reveals factors and forces that militate against the expression of ethics in educational leadership. History and the present illustrate that the multilayered qualities necessary for *being* ethical are not as embedded in educational leadership as they ought to be.

US History and Upside Down Ethics in Education

The history of US public education offers too many examples of upside down ethics. Ethics are turned upside down when terms and values that symbolize ostensibly ethical intentions or behaviors are inverted to promote bigotry, deliver discrimination, and instill hate.

Perhaps the most egregious example of this is the use of *freedom* to justify the denial of freedom. History recounts that Citizens' Councils were founded throughout the South during the mid-twentieth century in response to judicial mandates for school desegregation. These groups turned ethics and the founding principles of US democracy upside down and equated freedom with racism: "Segregation represents the freedom to choose one's associates, Americanism, state sovereignty, and the survival of the white race" (Suitts, 2019).

The racist intent of Citizens' Councils, vouchers, segregation academies, legislative initiatives, and private all-white schools created in several states to avoid the requirements of *Brown v. Board* (1954) demonstrate the crux of upside-down ethics. Proponents of a state plan in Alabama, for instance, argued for separation of the races by inventing a right of parents and caregivers to choose segregated schools:

> This parental liberty, like other liberties is not absolute; but is limited only by an overriding necessity for community order or welfare, reflected not in some remote Federal pronouncement, but in the grass-root exercise of state police power, by the State acting in its sovereign capacity. (Suitts, 2019)

The insidious character of upside down ethics is also captured in a report by a South Carolina commission established after *Brown v. Board* (1954). This report endowed local school leaders with the power of discrimination and unethical conduct by indicating "that, due to the US Supreme Court, there can be 'no racial segregation by law,' but nothing prohibited them from making 'assignment according to natural racial preference and the administrative determination of what is best for the child'" (Suitts, 2019).

Using ethics perpetrates an unethical environment on all students, school colleagues, and school communities when racism is portrayed as the moral equivalent of justice, freedom, or equality. The discriminatory objectives or goals camouflaged as integrity or fairness represent not only the history of unethical educational leadership but also portray aspects of twenty-first-century schooling.

PRESENT-DAY UPSIDE DOWN ETHICS

Upside down ethics are not an artifact buried in America's or public education's past. Scholarship, practice, politics, and ideology reveal the extent to which history repeats itself in US education. Three examples—(1) impact on students; (2) amorality of ideology; (3) *being* ethical is hard work—illustrate how upside-down ethics infect twenty-first-century education.

1) *Impact on students.* When school leaders neglect justice, caring, and the values of the moral obligation of public education, they allow their institution, their colleagues, and their professional practices to isolate, demean, or deny students and their capacities. Scholarship reveals significant negative effects on students when upside down ethics plague US schools:
    - Marginalization—Marginalization is treating another human being as insignificant. Students of color, students in poverty, and students whose first language is not English are often marginalized. Marginalization is the emotional, behavioral, and/or cognitive rendering "other" human beings peripheral.
    - Deficit thinking—When any adult assumes, without justification of any kind, that cohorts of students cannot be successful, teaching and other interactions demonstrate deficit thinking. Students subject to deficit thinking are abandoned; higher order learning becomes impossible and stereotype threat becomes endemic.
    - Racial opportunity cost—When students of color are subject to the assumption that they lack the capacities necessary and sufficient for school success, racial opportunity cost is levied. This assumption is levied to deny possibilities and potential; students who pay this cost feel its substantial price (Chambers, Huggins, Locke, and Fowler, 2014; Swensson and Shaffer, 2020).
    - Injustice, denial of social justice—"Social justice implies that persons have an obligation to be active and productive participants in the life of society and that *society has a duty to enable them to participate in this way*" (emphasis original) (Reisch, 2002, p. 346). Injustice is the denial of obligation, duty, or responsibility by any educator.
2) *Amorality of ideology.* Several ideological premises that can infect educational leadership—for example, free market theory; choice education; accountability via standardized testing—undercut the primary purpose and moral obligation of traditional US public education (Swensson, Ellis, and Shaffer, 2019b).

The ethical challenge presented by the ideology of free market theory is stark: a free market is amoral (Lubienski, 2013). Proponents of free market schooling celebrate efficiency instead of learning, mechanisms instead of teaching, and singularity instead of mutuality. Free market theory has no regard for and makes no provision concerning the welfare of students/consumers.

Frequently referred to as *neoliberalism*, free market theory "is characterized by faith in economic determinism, acquisitive individualism, entitlement ethics, and meritocracy" (Kurth-Schai, 2014, p. 423; Swensson, Ellis, and Shaffer, 2019a).

English (2005) adds that educational leadership anchored by free market theory "may be defined as a mindset that looks at all situations, interactions and potentialities as an economic exchange resulting in the maximization of profit" (p. 92).

Choice education and privatization create educational environments where amorality, marginalization, exclusion, and segregation are regular features (Shaffer and Dincher, 2020; Swensson, Ellis, and Shaffer, 2019a; Swensson and Shaffer, 2020).

3) *Being ethical is hard work.* Using ethics provides a path of least resistance to leadership that denies rights and respect to all students. *Being* ethical, on the other hand, puts school leaders in position to combat forces and factors that distort the values of the moral obligation of public education. *Being* ethical embodies the distinctive principles upon which US democracy was constructed. *Being* ethical is choosing the hard work and persistence that sustains virtue.

Singularity and the Hard Work of *Being* Ethical

WGOA (Who's the Greatest One of All) syndrome exemplifies a leader's choice of singularity. Singularity in this case is the active choice by leaders to forsake the intentions of ethics, purpose, and greater good in public education. Students, staff, community, and school are subordinated when leadership uses position, title, authority, and/or power for a singular purpose: to burnish the leader's image, wallet, personal desires, and/or prospects.

Leaders who embrace the WGOA syndrome evince choices and behaviors that have nothing to do with something greater than themselves. Instances of this infrequent but devastating syndrome and its unethical leadership occur when:

- the superintendent carries on a romantic affair with a subordinate;
- the principal arranges each spring for the school cafeteria to sell—in bulk at prices well below cost—hot dogs and hamburgers to school staff for their personal summertime consumption;

- the transportation director ensures that relatives and friends are favored with contracts if a percentage of the value of the contract ends up in the director's pocket;
- the team leader volunteers to sell concessions after school and "pockets" some of the cash received each afternoon;
- the assistant superintendent bypasses the Visitor ID process when entering school district buildings;
- the winningest coach in the school district helps him/herself to food and drinks at the school's concession stand;
- leaders, in many roles, expect that their school or school district "owes them" various perks (e.g., free admission to sports and arts events, free lunch in school cafeterias) in addition to their compensation package;
- the superintendent induces a member of the Board of Education to meet with a building leader and ask questions designed to trap the principal into participating in what the board member indicates is a "remove the superintendent" effort; and
- the principal asks for special treatment for their son/daughter in a teacher's class.

Leaders, in many roles, flaunt their title and position in professional relationships by violating policies or rules that all others in the school or school district are obligated to follow.

Unethical leaders enforce the singularity and self-aggrandizement they believe they so richly deserve.

Intimidation and veiled threats can be followed-up at the workplace by leaders who create difficult teaching/work schedules, or impugn a colleague's reputation, or pare a colleague's supply budget. The extent to which leaders make these choices, and the extent to which there is no or little systematic oversight of ethics, means that all who interact with leaders who create these environments are subject to the absence of virtue.

IS THERE A "HOW" OF *BEING* ETHICAL?

If *being* ethical were a metronome, leaders would have a ready-made rhythm upon which to base professional practice. Although there are values and principles widely recognized as the ethics that underlie leadership, no fail-safe backbeat is available from which leaders can synchronize their choices and behaviors with ethics.

The relationship between educational leadership and ethics, as a result, becomes intensely challenging and unremittingly vital because leadership is an unlimited responsibility to others. The challenge of *being* ethical lies within the fact that unlimited responsibility can be perceived as an oxymoron that prevents its own enactment.

Leaders are called to fulfill responsibilities to all others. But, to answer this call, the limitless potential responsibilities to hundreds or thousands of people creates an impossible situation for all school leaders "that limit[s] our ability to meet this challenge. In any multiple stakeholder environment, we are accountable to many different individuals, so how should we decide which of these different demands to prioritize" (Ciulla et al., 2017, p. 10).

Self-efficacy becomes a priority for educational leadership. School leaders who invest in function create the conditions and the agency for self-efficacy sufficient to the hard work of *being* ethical. Functions of leadership are an intentional and emergent social construction that explain how educators acquire what Bandura (1983) refers to as *perceived efficacy*.

Individuals gain these *self-precepts of efficacy* through "variable use of constituent skills under circumstances that differ in complexity, difficulty, or threat" (Bandura, 1983, p. 467). Constructing functions and enacting functions during professional practice constitutes a practical training ground for self-efficacy for functional educational leadership.

Integrity and *Being* Ethical

Alone an individual educator's self-precept of efficacy is necessary for function but not sufficient for function of leadership. In terms of ethics, an individual's integrity or lack of integrity rivets leadership to *being* ethical or to using ethics. Several dimensions of integrity including honesty or truth telling, trustworthiness, fairness, and conscientiousness (Van Wart, 2013, p. 560) provide leaders with feedback about *being* ethical. Additional insight into the "how" of *being* ethical is suggested by scholars who indicate that integrity is comprised of the ethics of justice and the ethics of caring.

- "The ethic of justice needs the profound commitment to the dignity of the individual person; [and]
- the ethic of caring needs the larger attention to social order and fairness if it is to avoid an entirely idiosyncratic involvement in social policy" (Stefkovich and Begley, 2007, p. 215).

A leader's ethic of justice and ethic of caring develop from "a great deal of self-reflection, open-mindedness, and an understanding that making ethically sound decisions profoundly influences others' lives" (Stefkovich and Begley, 2007, p. 215).

Leaders can judge their capacity for integrity by reflecting upon their own engagement with caring and justice. Sustaining integrity—based on self-reflection that takes account of personal integrity and how society perceives virtue—is the capacity leaders must learn, evaluate, and sustain to enact ethics as function of educational leadership. Under these circumstances, integrity, justice, and caring intermingle throughout the rungs of the double helix. Intentional enactment of functional educational leadership "enriches educational leaders' repertoire of skills in dealing with ethical issues" (Stefkovich and Begley, 2007, p. 215).

A DIFFERENT LEADERSHIP RESPONSIBILITY

A leader's responsibility for *being* ethical and the embedded responsibility for integrity constitute a leader's obligation to something greater than her/himself. Accepting this responsibility is a leader's acknowledgement that virtue and integrity are essential to the common good and that monitoring the pursuit of something greater than her/himself begins with the leader's self-efficacy. To assess the fulfillment of these responsibilities, educational leadership must attend to:

- Incorporating reflection to evaluate this rung in the double helix. A leader's monitoring of integrity depends upon

    personal reflection on the consequences of their own actions and on the desirability of those consequences to ensure that integrity is the foundation for relating practices to outcomes, for confronting the appropriateness of action for a particular situation (Mitchell et al., 1996, p. 57), and for linking new insights with prior understandings so as to reconstruct the school narrative. (Mitchell and Sackney, 2000, p. 20; Sackney and Mitchell, 2002, p. 902)

    A leader's ongoing reflection becomes "a meta-organizer and ultimate influence on their decision making" (Stefkovich and Begley, 2007, p. 206).
- Understanding their own grounding in ethics because (1) what a person values explains the motivation that shapes actions and attitudes, (2) what a leader values serves to guide responses to ethical dilemmas, and (3) ethics can be a mechanism to create consensus within a group for the pursuit of an organization's purpose or objectives (Stefkovich and Begley, 2007).

Reflection as Ethical Agency

Reflection creates open-mindedness which guides *being* ethical to focus on what all students deserve. Dewey (1933) captures the agency fostered by reflection when he indicates that reflection is a process that moves people away from routine ways of thinking about an experience and toward reflective action that involves "active, persistent and careful consideration" (p. 4).

When leaders engage in reflection, three attributes—rights, responsibility, and respect—guide ethics as a function through which leadership serves the best interests and well-being of all students (Stefkovich and Begley, 2007).

Rights are building blocks for ethics in leadership composed of the values of the moral obligation of public education, the Bill of Rights in the US Constitution, and the policies or statutes arising from these sources. These rights become *being ethical* when educators apply them during day-to-day decision-making, interactions, and dynamic instruction.

Responsibility is an individual's engagement with the unwritten social contract: "Everyone who received the protection of society owes a return for the benefit, and the fact of living in society renders it indispensable that each should be bound to observe a certain line of conduct toward the rest" (Stefkovich and Begley, 2007, p. 217).

Respect is the exercise of the responsibility to follow a positive line of conduct toward others. Respect under these circumstances is a mutual and positive interaction.

Integrity and its attributes are intentional choices. *Being* ethical, thus, is persistently a work in progress. The greater good of ethical leadership envisions "a democratic ideal of civic equality: individuals should be treated and treat one another as equal citizens regardless of their gender, race, ethnicity, race, religion, sexual orientation or socioeconomic status" (Gutmann and Ben-Porah, 2015, p. 5).

CHOOSING ETHICS INTENTIONALLY

For a school leader, *being* ethical day-to-day is either intentional, or it is not intentional. For example, virtue—a leader's relationship with ethics and competencies—is not a matter of happenstance. The function of ethics is intentional when school leaders take responsibility for the purposive self-mastery referred to as *internal accountability*.

Elmore (2005) relates that "the alignment of individual values with collective expectations, reinforced by the processes of accountability, results in internal accountability" (pp. 135–136). Lapsley (2008) refers to this as *self-mastery* that "is the conscious intentional process of gradually taking ownership ('colonizing') of various aspects of the self, including one's emotions, impulses, and dispositions" (p. 36).

Intentionality springs from a leader's choice of accountability to something greater than him/herself. The cause that Dewey mentioned as the North Star by which educators guide their professional journey becomes the motivator for ethical enactment of purpose and mission. The primary purpose of public education, the values of the moral obligation of public education, and the foundational principles of US democracy symbolize the greater good, the public good, for which educators must hold themselves and their colleagues accountable.

Alignment between these collective expectations and intentional leadership represents a leader's self-precepts of efficacy for ethics. Educational leadership that crafts intentionality for this internal accountability ensures that:

- greater skill is facilitated to focus the curriculum;
- staff are proficient problem solvers when determining the best instructional responses to the obstructions erected by performance measures;
- measures of performance are the province of local policy and practice aligned with locally identified core values (Elmore, 2005, p. 136; Swensson, Ellis, and Shaffer, 2019a).

Being ethical entails purposive self-mastery and internal accountability. "Moral leadership in schools seeks to bring members of that community together around common purposes in a manner that entails being deliberately moral (Dewey, 1932) in one's conduct—toward and with others and oneself" (Greenfield, 2004, p. 182).

DIRECT EFFECTS AND ETHICAL LEADERSHIP

Research confirms that school leaders have a positive effect on student achievement (Waters and Marzano, 2007) and "that the school leader's effects on students are almost entirely indirect (Day et al., 2009; Bosker, and Kruger, 2003)" (Seashore Louis, Dretzke, and Wahlstrom, 2010, p. 316). While these are valuable insights about the effects of school leadership including ethics, the direct effect of ethics or a lack of ethics in leadership deserve attention.

Direct Effects of *Being* Ethical

Public education generally, including the moral obligation of public education, is society's effort to make a difference in the lives of all students. This baseline is often taken at face value, however, without reflecting upon whether a difference for students' lives occurs. Although difference-making is often portrayed as a "'hope to change individuals for the better and to improve social conditions for all' (Foster, 1986, pp. 17–18)" (Greenfield, 2004, p. 184), how "better" is defined depends on educational leadership.

In terms of functional educational leadership, one measure of "better" is the growth of the capabilities that students bring from their lived experience.

Leading-out student capacities via dynamic instruction and ethics creates the evolution of a student's learning to gain the capacity of *freedom vis-à-vis learning* (Swensson and Shaffer, 2020).

Freedom vis-à-vis learning is cognitive, behavioral, and emotional engagement with critical habits of mind that strike the balance found in the social contract and positive liberty which yields the dynamic insight that "identity may be comprehensive without being all-encompassing" (Fraser-Burgess, 2012, p. 485; Swensson and Shaffer, 2020).

Freedom vis-à-vis learning facilitates a student's self-regulation, the ethical baseline from which a student does "not attach any sense of superior value to his cultural, ethnic, or racial identity but would instead see himself as a compound of several contingencies that make up the identity he had (Hill, 2000, p. 121)" (Reimers, 2006, p. 283).

Community and Ethics

Emerging from self-mastery, freedom vis-à-vis learning, and integrity is the presence of community. "The presence of community is essential because interactive dialogue is the only process available for generating shared standards and for achieving shared goals" (Sackney and Mitchell, 2002, p. 895).

Ethical leadership begins and ends as "we" and not as "I" (Sackney and Mitchell, 2002; Knight Abowitz, 2018; Swensson and Shaffer, 2020). The presence of "we" is a guide that informs leaders about their own actions and the extent to which intentionality successfully establishes the morality necessary for student-centric educational environments to thrive (Stefkovich and Begley, 2007).

The Moral Obligation of Public Education

Functional educational leadership exists only when ethics is one of the rungs in the double helix. Scholars offer an effective way to describe ethics as a leadership non-negotiable: "In educational administration, we believe that if there is a moral imperative for the profession, it is to serve the 'best interests of the student'" (Stefkovich and Begley, 2007, p. 212). The intentionality of *being* ethical is both necessary and sufficient to the educational environments that all students deserve.

LOOKING AT THIS CHAPTER IN THE REARVIEW MIRROR

Using ethics represents the antithesis of educational leadership. Functional leaders intend ethics because it is an essential element in the "how" of every other rung crafted for the doing of leadership in public education. Looking at this chapter in the rearview mirror provides the opportunity to reflect, in an open-minded way, on ethical school leadership:

- What are the forces and factors that make it so difficult for school leaders to be ethical at all times?
- Describe the circumstances and outcomes that you observed when an educational leader failed to be ethical. What, specifically, would you have done in that person's shoes to be ethical and what would have been the outcome compared with what actually happened?
- Paraphrase the importance of agency and action in the rung of "being ethical" that lies in the double helix representing functional educational leadership.
- Explain what you agree with and what you disagree with in this chapter; why do you take these positions?
- What should an educator do to influence the ethics of colleagues?

Chapter 7

Our Students Deserve—Emotionally Intelligent Leadership

Every student knows, and every adult remembers, that school is an emotional place. Individual emotions are wrapped up in learning. Interpersonal emotions are reflected in student–student, student–teacher, and adult–adult interactions. Emotions of the school community are expressed in pride, conflict, celebration, and crisis. Experience and reflection confirm that "the emotions are foundational to the way people experience their individual realities. This is as true in schools as it is elsewhere" (Beatty, 2000).

Despite the ubiquity of emotions in teaching, learning, and educational institutions, emotions have an incomplete presence at best in research about educational leadership. In response to a gap between what practitioners experience and what research incompletely clarifies, this chapter explores emotional intelligence (EI) in educational leadership.

What ought to be known about EI and the role of EI in leadership is examined in this chapter via these questions:

- Why is so little known about leadership and EI?
- Is there a relationship between rational intelligence and EI?
- What role does EI play in educational practice?
- What is the day-to-day leadership function of EI?

WHEREFORE ART THOU, EMOTIONAL INTELLIGENCE (EI)?

The emotions associated with teaching and learning in public schools, at first glance, appear to be fertile ground for research. Among the definitions of EI, Gray's (2009) straightforward scholarly statement resonates with practical significance: "emotional intelligence means having the ability to manage one's own emotions while being sensitive to the needs of other people" (p. 1). But clear and actionable statements like this are rare and cannot compensate for the largely indifferent scholarship about emotion and educational leadership.

Intelligence and Leadership: A Blast from the Past

The scholarship gap between emotion and educational leadership appeared with the dawn of the twentieth century. At that time, scholars like Henri Fayol and Frederick Taylor theorized how organizational leadership influenced efficient management in business and industry.

At about the same point in history, researchers initiated studies about the nature of intelligence. These theorists "defined intelligence as the global or composite capacity of an individual to act purposefully, to think rationally, and to deal effectively with the surroundings or situation" (Labby, Lunenburg, and Slate, 2012, p. 3). Rationality emerged as the conceptual and practical glue connecting efficiency and accountability with successful management of business and industry.

Indifference to Emotional Intelligence (EI)

Theories about leadership articulated a century ago and the professional practices derived from them continue to dominate practice and precepts of educational leadership. The study of EI and educational leadership is a lightly traveled research route (Labby, Lunenburg, and Slate, 2012, p. 2). The extent to which terms like *bureaucracy*, *management*, and *administration* are utilized in lieu of *leadership* in America's schools suggests how the past deters a functional understanding of school leadership and the emotions that suffuse it.

As practitioners know, rationality is necessary but not sufficient for leadership on behalf of educational environments that all US students deserve (Hoffman, Ivcevic, and Brackett, 2018). Because EI receives only cursory research attention, school leaders work with an incomplete map when they navigate the landscape of educational leadership.

LEADERS AND AN INCOMPLETE MAP

Although it's incomplete, the map that school leaders utilize includes several notable landmarks that suggest the presence of emotions in educational leadership.

Among these landmarks are prominent features identified by the earliest studies about organizational leadership: "Non-intellective elements were present that were as essential to intelligence as were the cognitive aspects" (Labby, Lunenburg, and Slate, 2012, p. 3). Even scholars such as "Thorndike (1920) defined social intelligence as the ability to manage and understand people" (Labby, Lunenburg, and Slate, 2012, p. 2).

Intimating more than rationality at the core of successful leadership, these early studies also spoke to "specific interpersonal skills (i.e., the ability to establish and maintain social networks; the ability to deal with subordinates; the ability to empathize with top-level leaders) as critical for managerial effectiveness" (Riggio and Reichard, 2008, p. 169).

The Behaviors of Emotional Intelligence (EI)

Although early research hints at interpersonal skills and emotion (e.g., tact, social skills, integrity, social intelligence) in leadership, scholars tended to follow in the research footsteps of rationality and "focused on behavior rather than consciousness" (Labby, Lunenburg, and Slate, 2012, p. 2). This tendency is illuminated in a summary of several studies about leadership that found "support for two broadly defined categories: task-oriented and relations-oriented behaviors" (Yukl, 2012, p. 67).

The purpose of task-oriented behaviors "is to ensure that people, equipment, and other resources are used in an efficient way to accomplish the mission of a group or organization" (Yukl, 2012, p. 69). Relations-oriented behaviors "enhance member skills, the leader-member relationship, identification with the work unit or organization, and commitment to the mission" (Yukl, 2012, p. 71).

Research anchored by behaviors puts rational intelligence at center stage for leadership and leaves emotion somewhere in the wings. Behaviors, after all, are observable; rational intelligence thrives on observability and the research manipulations that quantifiable observations permit. Allowing behaviors to suffice as if they alone identify, define, and determine the non-intellective elements of intelligence, however, is the research equivalent of looking at a prairie and determining that the earth is flat.

To avoid judging a globe by its prairies, educators require findings and insights generated from an understanding of intelligence as rational, emotional, and multidimensional. Moreover, although behaviors are one source for scholarly insights, behaviors are, at best, a research-proxy for consciousness. Largely unexamined, the relationship between leadership and consciousness and the extent to which EI functions in leadership are left to the imagination.

SOCIAL SKILLS: THE PEA UNDER THE LEADERSHIP MATTRESS

Rationality is the core of efficient leadership and this is confirmed—the essence of a self-fulfilling prophecy—when scholars do not inquire adequately about consciousness but can differentiate the effects of behaviors as the "emotional side" of rational intelligence. Explained away as charisma, talents "given" at birth, or the personality of a "great man," consciousness, social skills, and emotions of leadership are at the mercy of scholarship that renders EI anecdotal.

How Annoying! Emotions Interrupt Rationality

No matter how entrenched rationality, management, and bureaucracy became as paragons of organizational leadership, researchers continued to produce findings that hinted at emotions as a central player in intelligence and leadership. Researchers noted that "two leadership styles emerged: task versus consideration" (Labby, Lunenburg, and Slate, 2012, p. 5).

In this duality, *consideration* spotlights the role of social skills in effective leadership. "Consideration was defined as social-emotional leadership which was characterized by the friendliness and supportive mannerisms of the leader toward subordinates" (Labby, Lunenburg, and Slate, 2012, p. 5). Scholars also expanded upon the concept of intelligence to include—among other iterations—both intrapersonal and interpersonal intelligences (Gardner, 1983).

Intrapersonal intelligence is a person's comprehension of her/his individual emotions while interpersonal intelligence is an individual's abilities related to the emotions of others (Abrahams, 2007; Gardner, 1983). From this transformative insight, a scholarly conjunction between rational intelligence and EI unveils consciousness and consideration as integral to leadership.

Hypothesizing interconnectivity between intrapersonal and interpersonal intelligences, additional researchers advanced the understanding of emotion in intelligence (Abrahams, 2007). This nexus gained scholarly and practical acclaim when "Salovey and Mayer (1990) coined the term 'emotional intelligence' and defined it as 'the ability to monitor one's own and others' feelings, to discriminate among them, and to use this information to guide one's thinking and actions' (p. 189)" (Labby, Lunenburg, and Slate, 2012, p. 3).

As if to put an exclamation point behind the history of scholarship about leadership and intelligences, other scholars indicated that EI "is a multidimensional construct that is likened to verbal intelligence, or IQ" (Riggio and Reichard, 2008, p. 170).

A broad spectrum understanding of intelligence, thus, lends insight about the relationship between emotional intelligence (EI) and leadership. This more complete understanding is a development that incorporates additional scholarly perspectives including those of:

- Gardner (1983) who "took issue with using a single number, the intelligence quotient, to measure human intelligence" (Abrahams, 2007, p. 88);
- Sternberg (2017) who hypothesized that nonintellectual factors indicated the potential for human success; and
- Bar-On who "described emotional intelligences as the ability to work successfully with emotions or feelings and how to deal favorably with other individuals" (Labby, Lunenburg, and Slate, 2012, p. 3).

A leader's consciousness and consideration encompass "emotional skills [that] are related to the ability to accurately express, read, and understand emotions" (Riggio and Reichard, 2008, p. 170).

EMOTIONAL INTELLIGENCE (EI): A SET OF ABILITIES

On a day-to-day basis, the emotions inherent in teaching and learning can be affecting, alarming, annoying, comic, inspirational, and/or manipulative. The sheer volume of emotion can be deafening. At times, emotion-fatigue sets in; frustration with emotions can shut down the patience and professionalism required to enact EI.

EI as a function of educational leadership depends on intentionality. The intentionality of EI is the enactment of "the set of abilities (verbal and nonverbal) that enable a person to generate, recognize, express, understand, and evaluate their own, and others, emotions in order to guide thinking and action that successfully cope with environmental demands and pressures" (Van Rooy and Viswesvaran, 2004, p. 72).

Hoffman, Ivcevic, and Brackett (2018) identify a set of abilities delineated by four interrelated branches including "(1) perception and expression of emotion, (2) use of emotion to facilitate thinking, (3) understanding of emotions, and (4) management of emotion in oneself and others (Mayer and Salovey, 1997)" (p. 176).

The Ability Model of Emotional Intelligence (EI)

Identified in research as *the ability model of EI*, these four branches suggest the wide-ranging impact when EI functions throughout educational leadership. Each branch identifies intentionality for this function:

- The first ability in this model is the consciousness required to recognize emotions accurately and, from this recognition, to behave in a socially responsible way. Leaders, for example, can hone the ability to read "facial expressions, body language, vocal tone, and one's own physiological responses" (Hoffman, Ivcevic, and Brackett, 2018, p. 176). "Reading" the feelings or consciousness of others provides leaders with opportunities to act upon the emotions of others.
- Facilitating thinking using emotions—the second branch of the ability model—speaks to the intentional "application" of emotions by an individual when making decisions, thinking creatively, or focusing one's attention. Such purposeful use of emotions happens when leaders are adept at recognizing their own and others' emotions and the meaning of these emotions. This consideration of the role of consciousness is one way that educational leadership deliberately intertwines rational and EI to understand, guide, and improve educational environments and the interactions that occur within them.
- "The third ability—understanding emotions—encompasses recognizing the causes and consequences of how we feel and being able to assign a specific label to the experience" (Hoffman, Ivcevic, and Brackett, 2018, p. 177). This ability involves the capacity to know how complex emotions can be a combination of basic emotions. A leader's self-mastery is affected, for better or for worse, to the extent that causes, consequences, and labels for emotions can be recognized accurately.
- Finally, the fourth branch of the ability model of EI is a self-awareness or self-mastery in terms of both openness to one's emotions and in terms of interrelating all the abilities in this model to manage one's behavioral, intellectual, and/or emotional responses. Self-awareness or self-mastery also gives an educational leader the wherewithal to correlate or align responses with emotions that are applied to or that emerge with social construction.

The effect of this function of leadership is suggested by Beatty (2000) who observes that:

> interconnected emotional experiences of "what it's like around here" are organic, cumulative and foundational. They define, and redefine, in a continuous living psychodynamic gestalt, a collective knowing. And the principal is the biggest factor in the mix. This "knowing" combined over time with personal experiences, shapes and defines what happens inside and outside the people in schools.

EMOTIONAL INTELLIGENCE (EI) IN A LEADER'S DAY

EI is the "'ability to perceive emotions, to access and generate emotions so as to assist thought, to understand emotions and emotional knowledge, and to reflectively regulate emotions so as to promote emotional and intellectual growth' (Mayer and Salovney, 1997, p. 5)" (Gray, 2009, pp. 1–2). Daily, a leader's EI is a baseline from which interactions, feelings, and emotional reactions are deciphered. When school leaders enact EI as function, an emotionally intelligent school can develop.

Emotional Intelligence (EI) and the Limbic System

Enacting EI as function means accessing *the limbic system*. The limbic system is known as the brain's "control center" for human emotions.

The limbic system is referred to as an *open loop*. "An open-loop system depends largely on external sources to manage itself" (Goleman, Boyatzis, and McKee, 2004, p. 6). Scientists working to unravel the mysteries of the human brain indicate that "the open-loop design of the limbic system means that other people can change our very physiology—and so our emotions" (Goleman, Boyatzis, and McKee, 2004, p. 7).

The dependence of the limbic system on external sources for its management explains why a bully's taunting words are so emotional and why a student who is bullied often exhibits physiological symptoms like crying, expressing anger, or lashing out. Utilizing this same perspective, emotionally intelligent leadership constitutes an external source with the potential to affect the limbic systems of students, colleagues, parents/caregivers, and community members. A leader's EI, as a result, can either energize or demoralize a school or school district. Emotional intelligence suggests the ecology of functional educational leadership.

Emotional Intelligence (EI) and Academic Performance

Instruction shaped by the default culture loses connection with an expanding body of research that finds a connection between academic success and engaging students to be caring, self-regulated, and responsible (Hoffman, Ivcevic, and Brackett, 2018).

Student academic performance is enhanced when educational leadership intertwines emotional and rational intelligence. Scholars note that "social and emotional skills may be as critical for the basic knowledge repertoire of all children as reading, writing and arithmetic (Greenberg et al., 2004)" (Zeidner, Matthews, and Roberts, 2009, p. 227).

"Children with higher EI abilities have higher academic achievement than students with lower EI abilities (Ivcevic and Brackett, 2014; Manquez, Martin, and Brackett, 2006; Rivers et al., 2012)" (Hoffman, Ivcevic, and Brackett, 2018, p. 178). In addition, "researchers have found that prosocial behavior in the classroom is linked with positive intellectual outcomes (e.g.,

DiPerna and Elliott, 1999; Feshbach and Feshbach, 1987; Haynes, Ben-Avie, and Ensign, 2003; Pasi, 2001)" (Zins, Bloodworth, Weissberg, and Walberg, 2004, pp. 1–2).

Moreover, "emotions drive attention (Ohman, Flykt, and Esteves, 2001), and attention is key to memory and learning; anxious and angry students will likely have difficulty concentrating compared to their calm and happy peers" (Hoffman, Ivcevic, and Brackett, 2018, p. 178). When dynamic instruction puts students in a cognitive and emotional position to express their feelings through appropriate and clarifying language, "they are likely to receive more support and develop stronger relationships" (Hoffman, Ivcevic, and Brackett, 2018, p. 178).

Emotional Intelligence (EI) and Dynamic Instruction

The impact of EI and dynamic instruction on the learning and limbic systems of students can be fostered during SEL (social and emotional learning). SEL engages students with the values of the moral obligation of public education, social justice, and the principles of US democracy.

SEL is defined as a process through which human beings "'acquire and effectively apply the knowledge, attitudes, and skills necessary to understand and manage emotions, set and achieve positive goals, feel and show empathy for others, establish and maintain positive relationships, and make responsible decisions' (CASEL, 2013, p. 4)" (Hoffman, Ivcevic, and Brackett, 2018, p. 174).

As a factor in dynamic instruction and the development of self-mastery and amidst the socialization and social construction that occurs in any schoolhouse, SEL puts students in position to make judgments, based on their own reason, using thinking skills to attain mutuality and the values of the moral obligation of public education. SEL involves authentic and active learning to engage students to "care about others, make good decisions, behave ethically and responsibly, develop positive relationships, and avoid negative behaviors (Elias et al., 1997)" (Zins et al., 2004, p. 4).

Students in an emotionally intelligent school engage social and emotional habits of mind that are "non-cognitive skills (e.g., social skills, emotion regulation, persistence [that] are the best investment for adult productivity by fostering motivation, perseverance, and self-control) (Heckman and Masterov, 2007)" (Hoffman, Icevic, and Brackett, 2018, p. 175). Moreover, several studies indicate that SEL is associated with higher levels of student academic performance and fewer disciplinary concerns (Hoffman, Icevic, and Brackett, 2018; Ziedner, Matthews, and Roberts, 2009; Zins et al., 2004).

SEL facilitates school success measured beyond the limits imposed by rational intelligence. SEL, as part of the teaching and learning in the intersection of primary purpose and the moral obligation of public education, engages all students with cognitive, behavioral, and emotional school success that "must be defined far more broadly than as the scores students receive on standardized tests (Elias, Wang, Weissberg, Zins, and Walberg, 2002)" (Zins et al., 2004, p. 6).

Emotional Intelligence (EI) and Its Influence on Colleagues

On a day-to-day basis, a leader's strong EI has a positive effect on a wide array of interactions and communications, including:

- "The connection between teachers' confidence in their ability to do their job well and student performance" (Beatty, 2000).
- How colleagues perceive their school when school climate is an experience of "an emotional energy from the congruence of moral perspectives or moral purposes" (Beatty, 2000).
- "The will, the spirit, the desire to go on, the personal power to do one's best for self and other is a fundamentally emotionally driven phenomenon . . . [and] the wise leader knows this about her/himself, and about others, and respects the power potential for good or ill that lies therein" (Beatty, 2000).
- "Administrators who create the ongoing sense that teachers are supported, cared about and known, contribute tremendously to the emotional climate within which teachers must produce the conditions necessary for learning" (Beatty, 2000).

On the other hand, a leader's lack of EI can have a negative effect throughout an educational environment:

- Anger or a bad mood expressed by a leader toward a colleague tend to perpetuate themselves (Goleman, Boyatzis, and McKee, 2004).
- "A sour relationship with a boss can leave a person a captive of that distress with a mind preoccupied and a body unable to calm itself" (Goleman, Boyatzis, and McKee, 2004, p. 13).
- Distress or negative emotions are not only distractions but they erode both intellectual function and EI (Goleman, Boyatzis, and McKee, 2004).

THE VALUE OF EMOTIONAL INTELLIGENCE (EI)

The relationship between leadership and intelligence and how this relationship is understood has evolved. Leadership, beyond mere rationality, incorporates relations-oriented intelligence about behaviors that "increase the quality of human resources and relations, which is sometimes called 'human capital'" (Yukl, 2012, p. 68).

Scholarship about human capital—the quality of human resources and relations—explores the meaning and impact of "emotional literacy, the emotional quotient, personal intelligence, social intelligence, and interpersonal intelligence (Dulewicz and Higgs, 2000)" (Van Rooy and Viswesvaran, 2004, p. 72). As a result, research about and practice of educational leadership coalesced around the importance of "values such as, honesty, altruism, compassion, fairness, courage, and humility" (Yukl, 2012, p. 77).

In the growth of the sophistication of research about educational leadership lies the practical reality that school leaders no longer need be bound by the assumption that effectiveness depends on a forced choice between General Mental Ability (GMA) and EI. Informed by research about EI, school leaders need no longer be daunted by scholarly speculation that "it may be that EI is not a strong predictor of performance in and of itself" (Van Rooy and Viswesvaran, 2004, p. 73).

School practitioners now have confirmation of the day-to-day value of EI in the "research that shows that emotions and moods directly affect cognitive capability and performance in teams and organizations" (Abrahams, 2007, p. 89).

Leadership and the Emotionally Intelligent School

An emotionally intelligent school develops when leaders function from the understanding that they are "perhaps the single most defining variable in the energy balance of the school, an essentially emotional variable in the formula for school success" (Beatty, 2000).

Studies indicate that the emotional attributes enacted toward this end "include being adept at establishing effective relationships, developing productive teams, motivating employees, and transforming work environments" (Tench, 2016, p. 4). A resource accessible to all humans, "emotional intelligence (EI) is a set of skills that helps individuals reason with and about emotion" (Nathanson, Rivers, Flynn, and Brackett, 2016, p. 1).

The intentionality of functional educational leadership takes account of EI not only because this leadership is student-centric but also because this leadership enacts function (e.g., dynamic instruction, ethics) to thwart the human tendency to "island," tribalize, or impose singularity.

Leadership Choices and the Emotionally Intelligent School

A leader's choices constitute the agency of function. Emotionally intelligent leaders choose:

- *Social sensitivity:* Scholars confirm that "social sensitivity involves the ability to monitor one's own social behavior. This is closely related to the well-researched construct of self-monitoring (Snyder, 1974, 1987)" (Riggio and Reichard, 2008, p. 176). The inability or unwillingness of a leader to self-monitor leaves individuals, all staff members, and the school community emotionally and intellectually vulnerable.
- *Cultural sensitivity:* Culture is not a difference-blind construct. Fraise and Brooks (2015) correctly call attention to the fallacy "that characteristics and dynamics such as race, class, gender, and sexual orientation simply do not matter or that they are somehow not part of the concept of culture (Capper, 1993; Larson and Murtadha, 2002)" (p. 7). Empathy, respect, fairness—all symbolize the value of "the other" because positive difference-in-culture is at the heart of community, ethics, and emotion.
- *Emotional abilities:* Goleman (2011) identifies five components of EI that leaders can enact for success at work: self-awareness, self-regulation, motivation, empathy, and social skill (pp. 6–20).
- *Emotional DNA:* The abilities and components of EI mirror DNA in the human body because they enable leaders to "read" emotions. Just as educators know that thinking skills express rational intelligence, they know that social skills express EI. Social skills include "the ability to express oneself in social interactions, the ability to 'read' and understand different social situations, knowledge of social roles, norms, and scripts, interpersonal problem-solving skills, and social role-playing skills" (Riggio and Reichard, 2008, p. 171).
- *Social control:* Enacting leadership depends on the leader's *social control* which "is defined as skill in role-playing and social self-presentation and is perhaps the most critical leadership social skill" (Riggio and Reichard, 2008, p. 176). A leader who demonstrates tact and social competence incorporates social control in day-to-day practice as an element of self-mastery or self-regulation. "There is considerable evidence that the possession of social control is related to a sense of confidence and self-efficacy in social situations (Riggio et al., 1990)" (Riggio and Reichard, 2008, p. 176).

This understanding means that an emotionally intelligent school is one in which leaders are an *emotional guide*. The foremost task of EI as a function of educational leadership is "driving the collective emotions in a positive direction and clearing the smog created by toxic emotions" (Goleman, Boyatzis, and McKee, 2004, p. 5). In this way, EI can influence the open-loop of students, colleagues, and members of the school community. The open loop of the limbic system is subject to productive, constructive, and positive expressions of EI when this function intertwines with dynamic instruction and ethics in educational environments.

LOOKING AT THIS CHAPTER IN THE REARVIEW MIRROR

EI is a rung in the double helix of functional educational leadership. But EI is frequently disdained by or underrepresented in the extensive research about rational intelligence and leadership in education despite the significant role that emotions play in day-to-day educational environments. This odd juxtaposition of EI in practice and scholarship gives school leaders an uncertain platform upon which to build and grow their own EI in service to students, colleagues, and community.

This chapter suggests the difficulties and possibilities embodied by the emotional and rational intelligence required for effective leadership. The relationship between emotion and rationality within *leadership intelligence* deserves a great deal of further study. This relationship, furthermore, deserves to be cultivated, assessed, and nurtured during day-to-day professional practice by all school leaders.

There are several questions that readers can use to explore their own sense about practice associated with the meaning of this relationship:

- Which aspects of the scholarship cited in this chapter will you add to your application of EI in your daily professional practice? Explain your answer.
- Reflect on one of your own professional experience with emotion(s). Discuss the ideas shared during this chapter that add insight to your reflection that you wish you had been able to incorporate at the time.
- Write an explanation of EI and how it can be "applied" professionally. Share your ideas (verbally or in writing) with colleagues.
- Return to the questions posed in the introduction to this chapter; what are your answers based on the material you've read?

Chapter 8

Our Students Deserve— Public Life Education

There is a long-standing relationship between US democracy and traditional public education (Dewey, 1916; Swensson and Shaffer, 2020). This is a mutually beneficial relationship often represented in the term *citizenship education*. Public education was founded in US democracy; public education informs and empowers citizens for participation in US democracy.

In a simpler era, examples of citizenship education included displays of patriotic artwork, required courses in US History and Government, or reciting the Pledge of Allegiance to start each school day. From these and other expressions and experiences, an intended outcome of public education was positive manifestations of citizenship by US adults.

In a more complicated American society frequently defined by fragmentation, however, the relationship between public education and citizen participation is less apparent.

Although citizenship for democracy continues to be part of the routine in US public schools, cohesion amidst diversity, justice for all, and behaviors that advance the principles framed by the Constitution and Bill of Rights elude many individuals. As a result, connections between students and democratic principles espoused in America's founding documents, activated by respect for the rule of law, and summarized by the nation's motto *e pluribus unum* (from many, one) atrophy (Swensson, Ellis, and Shaffer, 2019b). Participation in and allegiance to democracy erode.

As citizenship education and its impact in US democracy waver, two benefits are lost and thrown into stark relief:

- First, democracy flourishes when citizens learn to participate.
- Second, all citizens benefit when education fosters the enlightened self-interest that undergirds respect, social justice, and the mutuality of participation in democracy.

When the connections between US public education and democracy unravel, two dilemmas loom:

- First, the absence of an effective relationship between learning and citizenship is a vacuum in which principles antithetical to democracy flourish.
- Second, as this relationship comes apart, students—America's future voters and citizenship participants—are less attached to the rationales for citizenship participation in US democracy.

Under these conditions, irony makes a disturbing appearance. At the same time, the long-standing intentions of the relationship between citizenship education and democracy erode, US public schools have become "one of the few social settings through which diverse citizens can interact in sustained and meaningful ways to achieve common goals" (Kurth-Schai, 2014, p. 427).

Just as the relationship between public education and US democracy erodes, it becomes an ever more essential bulwark against the erosion of citizenship participation. Irony, in this instance, constitutes a warning for US public educators and democracy.

The purpose of this chapter is to put readers in position to understand this warning. This warning alerts US school leaders that a first-tier objective now appears to be required before engaging students with citizenship education. This first-tier objective will be referred to throughout this discussion as *public life education*.

The fundamentally altered relationship between democracy and public education is a challenge to school leaders. Readers will encounter several waypoints during this chapter that examine this challenge and the rung in the double helix that meets the challenge head-on:

- The erosion of citizenship education.
- A school leader's approach to public life.
- The not-so-funny thing that happened on the way to citizenship education.
- The phenomenon of *islanding*.
- A transformational function of educational leadership: public life education.
- DCaR and the public thing we're looking for.

THE EROSION OF CITIZENSHIP EDUCATION

One intention of American public education is clear. Public schools in the United States intend to engage students with citizenship education to sustain and nourish the common good of the principles of democracy.

The originators of America's Common Schools (the first US public schools created in the 1800s) foresaw citizenship education for the common good as a primary objective. "The goal of these schools wasn't just to teach young people to internalize democratic norms but also to make it possible for capitalism to coexist with republicanism" (Labaree, 2018, p. 10).

Almost two centuries later, however, citizenship education and the common good face an uphill battle to remain as a fundamental goal of US public education. A variety of factors erode student engagement with the mutual benefits intended by this fundamental goal. Among these factors, social scientists identify a significant decrease in civic engagement or *social capital* (Putnam, 1993). Too often, Americans have little involvement with the "features of social organization, such as networks, norms, and trust, that facilitate coordination and cooperation for mutual benefit" (Putnam, 1993, p. 2).

The daily lives of US students involve few connections with the activities or allegiances that foster an understanding of social capital, mutual benefit, compromise, or fairness. The lived experience of US students as the twenty-first century moves forward lacks engagement with the capacities for *public life*.

Public Life and Mutuality

Public life is an expression of social capital that entails unity, improvement, and mutuality amidst difference and disagreement. "Public life will never be able to dispense with antagonism for it concerns public action and the formation of collective identities. It attempts to constitute a 'we' in a context of diversity and conflict (Mouffe, n.d., para. 4)" (Knight Abowitz, 2018, p. 2).

One element of public life of notable value in education is *collective identity*, the important concept articulated by Ogbu (2004). Ogbu (2004) speaks to the history of collective identity for African Americans in the expression and embrace of pride in being black that was socially constructed during the late twentieth century. This we-feeling was "a new public and psychological acknowledgement [in] the expression of Black collective identity" that reached across all segments of Black America (Ogbu, 2004, p. 18). Collective identity, as shared here, plays a vibrant role in the lived experience and I identify as . . . statements of African Americans.

Collective identities and "we," in the context referenced above by Knight Abowitz (2018), intertwine as public life. Public life is "not the seeking of unanimity or harmony, but rather, a meeting of different, independent perspectives emerging 'from the heart of life in all its expansive and messy disarray, not as consensus, but as a comingling of viewpoints'" (Cuilla et al., 2018, p. 9).

A snapshot of what can be described as the comingled reality of US demographics demonstrates the worth of public life education: during the decade from 2003 through 2013, "the percentage of White students in public elementary and secondary schools decreased from 59% to 50%, whereas percentages of Hispanic and Asian/Pacific Islander students increased from 19% to 25% and 4% to 5%, respectively (Kena et al., 2016)" (Minkos et al., 2017, p. 1260).

School Leadership and Public Life

The viability of the relationship between public education and American democracy faces difficulties in the present-day during the age of accountability. Can existing paradigms for citizenship education suffice (1) when voters and everyone associated with public education are frequently treated as if they are mere customers (Boyte, 2013), and (2) when so little of the lived experience of American students incorporates public life?

Furthermore, are school leaders content with what appears to be the anemic state of citizenship education? Can educational leaders improve citizenship education if collective identity and "we" are not intentional throughout public education?

Public Education: A Habit of Public Creation

The answer to these questions lies in the determinate capacities chosen by school leaders to "generate the sense of agency and larger civic imagination" (Boyte, 2013, p. 6) that symbolizes the core of public life. The extent to which educational leadership during the remainder of the twenty-first century develops and expresses these capacities will likely be determined by the extent to which leaders adopt and adapt what Knight Abowitz (2018) refers to as *habits of public creation*.

Habits of public creation "include communication, or building a sense of the 'we,' trusting others in shared forms of leadership and knowledge-building, empowering others as publics build capacity to make change, and transcending individualistic frames of knowledge and action (Knight Abowitz, 2014)" (Knight Abowitz, 2018, p. 11). Habits of public creation are intentional and agentic.

Habits of public creation acknowledge and value collective identity as "people's sense of who they are, their 'we-feeling' or 'belonging'" (Ogbu, 2004, p. 3). A resource for the evolution of democracy, an individual's engagement with cherished identity, and an invitation for mutual understanding of difference, collective identity becomes what should be known as a *learnable moment* if function guides and empowers educational leadership.

Habits of public creation put educational leaders in position to resolve "'the issue between a system that promotes the will of all and one that advances the idea of a true public, where private interest is put aside for the sake of discovering and advancing the common good' (Feinberg, 2012, p. 5)" (Kurth-Schai, 2014, p. 431).

A FUNNY THING HAPPENED ON THE WAY TO CITIZENSHIP EDUCATION

Individuals engage with mutuality through experiences in public life. Two terms, *the common good* and *the public good*, are used interchangeably to describe these experiences and the mutuality that they evoke. The common good and the public good are the shared benefits created when individuals interact as the public to establish balance of mutuality (Knight Abowitz and Stitzlein, 2018).

The benefits of mutuality include behaviors aligned with the social contract. These behaviors originate as an intelligence spawned in public life. This intelligence—referred to as *the intelligence of social balance* (Swensson and Shaffer, 2020)—is the intricate understanding conveyed in a simple metaphor: choosing to pay the "cost" of limiting individual arm-swinging while walking down the sidewalk to earn, in return, the universal benefit of no broken noses.

If they rarely experience mutuality, the common good, or the intelligence of social balance, then US students lack many of the foundational understandings (e.g., the Golden Rule; compromise; fairness) upon which citizenship education can be constructed. As the life experiences of many US students become ever more disconnected from characteristics that herald public life, social capital, and a readiness for citizenship education, US public education has less traction to reach a fundamental goal. This dilemma suggests that a preliminary objective must bolster students' intelligence of social balance before engaging with citizenship education.

Islanding: Land's End for the Intelligence of Social Balance

Before freedom, compromise, civic engagement, and the public good are hammered together as the intelligence of social balance for citizenship education, public educators must respond to the centrifugal experiences that students "collect" and bring to school.

The degree of difficulty that always attends educational leadership is magnified because public life itself is less available to, and less sought by, individuals separated on digital and ideological islands. For "I" and "we" to coalesce with the principles of democracy in the intelligence of social balance amidst robust diversity and shared humanity, educational leadership must account for *islanding*.

If Everyone Is an Island

Twenty-first-century relationships and communications manifest a tendency for individual priorities and differences to take precedence over, and demand distance from, the public good. Individual interests, further, often constitute the valorization of exclusion of and discrimination toward "other" identities.

Individual interests are the disassembled crux of many present-day social relationships. Moreover, social relationships have morphed into screenshots, video or snapped chats, instant/brief messaging of different kinds, and/or deliberate disconnection represented in shaming, revenge media, social media hate, and/or online bullying. Singularity (thinking and acting exclusively for self-aggrandizement of individuals or cohorts) excludes "the other."

Public life is disdained by those who claim preeminence for their own perspective. Such a denial of virtue and such denigration of the beneficial mutuality generated in the relationship between democracy and public education is nothing less than the shroud of disconnection endemic to islanding.

The Premise of *Islanding*

Islanding is the oxymoronic premise of one individual that he/she is a priority at all times and in all circumstances and that other individuals are not. Islanding is reinforced by social media's separation-effect but islanding is not a product of digitization alone. Islanding is singularity that takes shape as a group phenomenon, an individual affectation, and/or an educational infestation.

Islanding: A Group Phenomenon

Islanding is a group phenomenon when self-identified cohorts reject and debase humans they identify as "others" because of race, religion, gender orientation or identity, nationality, ethnicity, or any other factor that differs from the group who asserts the self-assigned privilege inherent in group-islanding.

The world's history flows into the present in countless waves of group-islanding. China's internment of the Uyghurs, France's discrimination against Muslims, Myanmar's brutalization of the Rohingya, America's mistreatment of a lengthy list of racial, religious, and ethnic "others"—all illuminate group-islanding that rejects, excludes, and denigrates. As a group phenomenon, islanding is the propensity to adopt *us vs. them* as if this justifies the imposition of hegemony by an us-group over a them-group.

Islanding: An Individual Affectation

Islanding is an individual affectation when self-aggrandizement is a person's first and only thought or behavior. Individuals employ islanding to separate themselves from common purposes and the public good. Such a separation is an individual's escape from the perceived impediments of self-mastery, the social contract, or democracy. The common good is disdained because it delays or denies personal gratification, preferred choice, or exclusive rights.

Islanding is an individual affectation without regard for mutuality; there is no need for the intelligence of social balance when an individual's needs are the sole imperative for that individual. The self-serving self-importance of islanding eschews public life and the principles of democracy.

Islanding: An Educational Infestation

Islanding is the assumption of a "right" to assert primacy or dominance over other individuals. Islanding and its singularity infest the history of US education and continue into present-day through the dedicated efforts of free marketeers (Swensson, Ellis, and Shaffer, 2019b). Free market or choice education proponents are the marketeers who invert the relationship between education and democracy with the result that segregation results (Shaffer and Dincher, 2020). The assumption that singularity takes precedence over mutuality and public life, and the imposition of exclusion of "the other" is the intent of this infestation.

Educational islanding is manifest further when interactions between educators and students are replaced by technology. There can be immense value in the use of technology as a tool to further the application of habits of mind during active learning crafted by the original power of education. But assuming the richness of dynamic instruction or the exchange of ideas that constitutes the original power of education are replicated or exceeded through technological substitutes is as misguided as assuming an avatar is a human being.

Flipped classrooms, 1:1 computer initiatives, and virtual schooling are scenarios too often devoid of creativity, insight, cognition, and interaction engaged through authentic learning. Such instructional deserts are often mass-marketing approaches that lack checks and balances for the integrity and quality of both curriculum and instruction. Many students left to their own devices in these low-engagement, thoughtless educational environments, disengage from learning. Under these conditions, citizenship education has little impact on America's students.

PUBLIC LIFE EDUCATION: A TRANSFORMATIONAL LEADERSHIP FUNCTION

The challenges of islanding and disconnection presented by islanding change the landscape for teaching and learning in ways that seem to have snuck up on twenty-first-century public educators. It was once effective to position citizenship education as the first and best step into participation in democracy. Without a foundation of lived experience with public life, however, students now have little or no foundation from which to construct their own habit of public creation: citizenship participation.

Citizenship education has become just another point of disconnection for students who have no grasp of the characteristics, principles, or behaviors of public life. Under these circumstances, school leaders have choices to make: transform and improve US democracy or allow islanding to further encroach on mutuality, social justice, and citizenship.

Enacting a Transformation

When educational leaders make choices, improvement and transformation are possible but not inevitable. The responsibilities of educational leaders in US democracy to foster environments that engage all students with the intelligence of social balance—for example, mutuality, fairness, respect, social justice—cannot be met during the remainder of the twenty-first century unless a transformational choice is made.

The choice that lies before school leaders is whether to choose a new first-tier learning experience before engaging students in citizenship education. This first-tier learning experience is a leadership choice to valorize collective identity alongside the mutuality of "we" in public life. This choice establishes a function of educational leadership that will be referred to as *public life education*.

Functional educational leadership continues to be responsible for envisioning and enacting public schools that are "places of interactive learning and building social relationships. To be successful, they must accommodate individual interests and differences in a way that also meets society's common needs and promotes certain shared values and principles" (Knight Abowitz and Stitzlein, 2018, p. 34). This responsibility is a challenge to school leaders because students often lack readiness for citizenship education crafted by socialization in public life.

Public life education becomes the transformation of educational environments that engages student meaning-making with habits of mind, behaviors, and experiences of public life. Public life education is rooted in the conjunction of "we," collective identities, and I identify as . . . statements.

The conjunction of these elements depends on leadership that intentionally transforms the islanding that immobilizes present-day citizenship education. Public life education engages all students with the intersection of how to think and the moral obligation of public education to accommodate and explore the encounters and mutuality of public life that many US students do not experience before attending public school.

PUBLIC LIFE EDUCATION AND DEMOCRACY

Public life education proceeds from the premise that although socialization will always be part of the unwritten curriculum, socialization ought to be influenced on behalf of mutuality of US democracy via the intentionality of educational leadership. Public life education puts educational leadership in position to nurture collective identity, valorize "we," and rectify the centrifugal tendencies that separate citizens from participation in US democracy.

In the twenty-first century, individual goods and public goods depend on public life encounters fostered by public things. Public things "are those material objects and spaces that are a shared and intractable part of democratic life" (Knight Abowitz, 2018, p. 8). Traditional public education is a public thing.

The nature of function in US public education is the creation of *the good* as a shared and intractable part of democratic life. *The good* represents, among other things, the values of the moral obligation of public education and the principles of US democracy. *The good* becomes shared and intractable if educational leadership commits to responsibilities and obligations inherent in public life education. These include but are not limited to:

- *Principled reasoning, the intelligence of common ground, and positive liberty*: These are among the capabilities students acquire when functional educational leadership leads to comprehensive public education (Swensson and Shaffer, 2020). Functions in educational leadership support the creation of public things where the principles of democracy and values of the moral obligation of public education are made manifest.
- *Freedom vis-à-vis learning*: This is the capacity for intelligence of common ground exemplified in the behaviors, choices, and problem-solving that

represent the social contract and positive liberty (Swensson and Shaffer, 2020).
- *Dynamic instruction*: This function is a symbolic thing of lasting civic value because it exerts the original power of education to strengthen and build the cognitive, emotional, and behavioral capacities for public life and, eventually, civic education. Dynamic instruction offers "meaning, a sense of permanence, and self-definition" (Knight Abowitz, 2018, p. 9) to every student.

The commitment of educational leaders to *the good* is a commitment to public life education. From this commitment, students acquire capabilities required to participate in the liberties, freedoms, and responsibilities of citizenship in a democracy (Gutmann and Ben-Porah, 2015; Swensson and Shaffer, 2020). Public life relies upon and evinces these capabilities in the form of and agency by "free and equal individuals" (Gutmann and Ben-Porath, 2015, p. 2).

Public Life Education and Dissent

Dissent is an aspect of democracy that function accommodates as a characteristic of social construction. Dissent is the right to hold opinions or ideas that vary from those generally held. Agency attends this right; dissent, in democracy, confronts the majority. Dissent is participation in public life with points of view that are not held in common. A leader's accommodation of dissent becomes a habit of public creation.

Democracy, public life, and citizenship are subject to and products of dissent. This means that public life education cannot function as an academic pathway to sameness, the status quo, or enforced agreement. Instead, public life education—like all habits of public creation—is the function that enacts encounters with differences of opinion, professional disagreements, compromise, personality conflicts, collaboration, misunderstandings, and deliberate affronts.

These encounters are, unto themselves, social constructions comprised of give-and-take, back-and-forth, and dissent-and-disagreement that are inevitable in public life.

Conflict may parallel dissent. Conflict, in terms of public life education, is a nonviolent struggle over opinions, ethics, procedures, processes, objectives, or goals undertaken with intensity. Confrontation is participation in conflict; functional educational leadership is the exercise of habits of public creation on behalf of resolution that serves the mutuality of democracy.

The Gist of Public Life Education

Public life education is the foundation required by the exigencies of the twenty-first century if citizenship education is to have its intended impact necessary to preserve and improve US democracy.

Functional educational leadership and the cycle of *dissent, conflict, and resolution* (DCaR) are habits of public creation that take account of *propriespect*, "the notion that every single person experiences culture differently" (Fraise and Brooks, 2015, p. 10). Instead of reacting as if difference is incompatible with public life, public life education embraces *propriespect* and DCaR. This cycle incorporates the intelligence of social balance and common ground to valorize collective identity and the value of "we."

DCaR and Functional Educational Leadership

DCaR comingles viewpoints; collective identity and "we" are mutuality when educational leaders pay attention to:

- *"I" with "we."* Public leadership engages colleagues and students with the original power of education as one means to encounter "I" and "we" in public life. As illustrated earlier, "we" is necessary to bring a multitude of principles of US democracy into the agency of engagement and participation. Educators must also understand that "I" is equally necessary. In this instance, "I" is wrapped up in *I identify as . . . statements* articulated by each student as their expressions of evolving lived experience (Swensson, Ellis, and Shaffer, 2019b). Just as individuals express many more than one self-understanding within these statements (Swensson, Ellis, and Shaffer, 2019b; Swensson and Shaffer, 2020), public life education mirrors the resilience of social construction for nurturing and abiding collective identities and I identify as . . . statements within the "we" of public life in US democracy.
- *Trust.* Trust is a "reciprocal process [that] can build on itself with the occurrence of more frequent trusting interactions between individuals, which may ultimately affect the entire system, thereby creating a sense of collective trust" (Daly, 2009, pp. 174–175). Daly (2009) invokes the mutuality of "benevolence, competence, integrity, openness, reliableness, and respect" (p. 175) at the center of trust-based interactions.
- *Systems.* A system is a set of things, ideas, and/or people functioning together to achieve purposes or goals. When leaders articulate the purposes for functioning together in a school or school district, a foundation is created for the systems of public life. Creations of public habit result in systems that conjoin trust and collective identity with "I" and "we" for the greater good.
- *Improvement.* Systems are subject to internal and external forces. How these forces influence public education depends on leadership. Leadership inaction in response to these forces often means that *dysfunction* is not far behind. Taking responsibility when a habit of public creation is subject to

these forces, however, means that leadership functions on behalf of *continuous improvement* within system.
- *Presence.* The mission statement of a famous fish market in Seattle highlights the fundamental notion that *being present* is key to job success because being present means relating to people as human beings. To *be present*, educators everywhere must recognize what leaders in small and rural schools know: that community is where "personal and working relationships are intimate, complex, and multidimensional (Arnold, 2004; Arnold et al., 2005; Kannapel and DeYoung, 1999; Lamkin, 2006)" (Forner, Bierlein-Palmer, and Reeves, 2012, p. 2). Presence is the opposite of singularity. Presence is associated with both public life and emotional intelligence.
- *Dissent.* Public life education is where dissent is an opportunity for learning. "Dissent is as necessary to well-functioning democracy as is consensus (Stitzlein, 2013), although the dissent is not between enemies, but between adversaries—the opponents with whom one shares commitment to general democratic principles" (Knight Abowitz, 2018, p. 6). Functional educational leadership in schools and school districts, then, is committed to dissent that occurs between adversaries.

THE PUBLIC THING WE'RE LOOKING FOR

In the face of singularity, exclusion, and the erosion of the relationship between public education and citizenship education, school leaders search for *public things*. As it turns out, the public thing missing from educational leadership is the philosophical and professional space required to enact citizenship education.

Educational leadership, as this discussion suggests, does not have the necessary influence on citizenship education because a first-tier space is required before citizenship education can be realized. This first-tier space is the common ground of public life that too many US students lack. Greenfield's (2004) conception of the *intelligence of common ground* symbolizes the worth of public life education as this first-tier space.

Intelligence of common ground becomes space for building a moral community from autonomy, connectedness, and transcendence while communicating about justice, critique, and care as the elements in the framework of ethics that support and sustain the school as a community (Greenfield, 2004, p. 181). Common ground, common purpose, and the common good emerge when dynamic instruction builds these elements into teaching and learning in educational environments.

Of greater consequence, habits of public creation undertaken through function by school leaders represent the public thing of greatest consequence to the future of all students: the principles of US democracy. Functional educational leadership enacts public life education as a public space where students acquire the competencies and capabilities for successful adulthood in US democracy.

LOOKING AT THIS CHAPTER IN THE REARVIEW MIRROR

The intentionality of functional educational leadership is an incubator for mutuality. Capacities necessary and sufficient for the accommodation of individual interests/differences and common needs/shared principles throughout public life are foundational to the relationship between public education and US democracy. Students engaged with public life education participate in determinate educational environments where learning fosters public life on behalf of a future where citizenship participation, social justice, and mutuality thrive.

Public life education empowers student capacity for comingling viewpoints. In this way, public life education is a function of school leadership that persistently pursues what *should be known* as the impetus for continuous improvement of US public education. Public life education pulls together individuals and eschews the singularity of islanding. These questions put the reader in position to accommodate the primary intentions of this chapter:

- How do the elements of DCaR represent the intents and outcomes of public life education?
- List the responsibilities of educational leadership that are mentioned throughout this chapter. Explain for each of these why you do, or do not, agree that these obligations are appropriate for school leaders.
- Put in your own words an explanation of these terms from this chapter: "we" ... *propriespect* ... habit of public creation ... collective identity ... mutuality. What do these concepts have to do with educational leadership as it's portrayed in this chapter?
- Describe how you would begin to implement public life education in your school. Include in your description how citizenship education is currently dealt with in your school.
- Why is *islanding* a powerful phenomenon and what examples of *islanding* have you experienced in your career?

Chapter 9

Enacting Functional School Leadership

School leaders have several options when considering whether to put function into practice. The first option is to choose to do nothing to enact functional educational leadership. The tendency of an organization to sustain its status quo is well-documented. Transforming the status quo of educational leadership is a notoriously difficult enterprise.

The next option that educational leaders can consider is to retrench or "transform backward." This option involves dismantling public education. In place of present-day educational leadership and the institutions it serves, the ethos that guides this option for schooling is dedicated to singularity instead of public life. Present-day marketeers and their ilk offer the destruction of public education as a choice (Swensson, Ellis, and Shaffer, 2019b).

The third option for public school leadership is the most difficult choice. But this option offers the prospect of transformation to fulfill the purpose and obligations of traditional public education. This option is the enactment of *functional educational leadership*.

This chapter grapples with how educational leaders enact function. Functions of educational leadership are a leader's intention to focus on primary purpose, moral obligation, and the original promises of traditional public education aligned with the principles of democracy. The enactment of function of school leadership will be examined through a discussion that incorporates:

- A return to the indeterminate zone of educational leadership.
- Accountability reimagined.
- The echo chamber of present-day educational leadership.
- Function and the construction of educational leadership.
- A picture of functional educational leadership.
- How to function as an educational leader.

A RETURN TO THE INDETERMINATE ZONE OF EDUCATIONAL LEADERSHIP

The indeterminate zone of educational leadership pictured in figure 3.1, the singularity visited upon lived experience, and the echo chamber built by standardized testing, leave educational leaders with few clues about the nature of function. More vague, from a leader's point of view, is how to put function into daily practice.

Marbles Throughout the Indeterminate Zone

The models, theories, expectations, standards, practices, and styles that surround leadership in the indeterminate zone stick together like marbles on an incline. Rolling away from coherence, these concepts ensure that present-day educational leadership is unreliable. The degree to which educational leadership can be depended upon to engage all students accurately with the learning they deserve is low.

In the indeterminate zone, educational leadership is vulnerable. Not only is stasis a regular outcome from this vulnerability but vulnerability, itself, invites the dysfunction of free market theory to substitute where *leading-out* and the original power of education ought to hold sway. When the indeterminate zone nurtures the first two options for educational leadership, function, purpose, and promises in US public education slip and slide away.

Unable to perform consistently well, educational leadership mimics the irresolute nature of the indeterminate zone:

- Goldring et al. (2007) postulate school leadership at the confluence of six core components and six key processes. This mélange of leadership is envisioned as delivery mechanisms for the standards embedded in *No Child Left Behind Act* (NCLB) legislation. This perspective assumed that NCLB would force school leaders to assemble a rigorous curriculum and develop quality instruction. Instead, the opposite ravaged teaching and learning throughout US public schools. The equivalent of ideological smoke and mirrors (Ravitch, 2020), NCLB and all the counterproductive educational gizmos that exist in its wake force educational leadership to eschew reliability in favor of compliance.
- Accreditation and accountability standards for educational leadership tend to be vague, assumptive, and restrictive. For example, ISLLC Standard 2 indicated that an educational leader sustains "a school culture and instructional program conducive to student learning and staff professional growth" (Murphy, 2003, p. 44). But standards leave the nature of learning

and growth to the wiles of the "fittest" political player in the game which, disastrously, has been and continues to be standardized testing.
- Even fast-forwarding to NELP (National Educational Leadership Preparation) Standards, which the National Policy Board for Educational Administration (NPBEA) indicates "are aligned to Professional Standards for Educational Leadership (PSEL)" (NPBEA, n.d.) does little to engage school leaders with function. NELP Standards are focused on accreditation of university educational leadership preparation programs while PSEL Standards (formerly referred to as ISLLC Standards) (NPBEA, 2015) embody glittering educational generalities. For example, PSEL Standard 4a notes that "effective leaders implement coherent systems of curriculum, instruction, and assessment that promote the mission, vision, and core values of the school, embody high expectations for student learning, align with academic standards, and are culturally responsive" (NPBEA, 2015, p. 12).

To enact function, school leaders must intend that the primary purpose of public education and the moral obligation of public education are nonnegotiable objectives. Moreover, "how" function of leadership occurs cannot be left to generalities; instructional function, as illustrated in this discussion, places a premium on the engagement and practice that all students deserve from public education's leadership. This determination initiates each leader's agency to deconstruct the indeterminate zone of educational leadership.

Out of the Zone and into the Accountability Fire

Ridding public education of the indeterminate zone's encirclement is only the first task that must be undertaken to serve all US students in the educational environments that they deserve. The second task that public educators must take on and that school leaders must prioritize is action that involves jumping out of the proverbial frying pan but avoiding the fire set by free market theory and standardized accountability.

Choice is a ubiquitous, powerful, and misleading example of a silver bullet that critics aim at traditional public schools and educational leadership. Choice (facilitated by free market theory mechanisms such as charter schools, vouchers, and tax abatement) assumes that efficiency and accountability (engineered via standardized testing and sanctions assigned to schools based on results from these tests) allow "parents to remove their children from schools receiving low grades [and that] will ultimately ensure that only high-performing schools survive" (Murray and Howe, 2017, p. 4).

Like all other panaceas, however, choice is an educational unicorn. The supposition that accountability is inseparable from free market schooling and, as a result, that students will receive a better education because accountability guarantees school excellence is nothing less than mystical thinking.

Murray and Howe (2017) examined the processes and data utilized to make judgments about schools based on test results and found that "the selection and weighting of criteria seem to have no basis other than the seat-of-the-pants intuitions of policymakers woefully lacking in technical knowledge and skills" (p. 7).

In addition, grades given to schools are concoctions of interpreted data that are incomplete at best and misleading at worst. An "empirical analysis of Oklahoma school grades revealed, for example, that there were practically no differences in average science and reading scores among 'A,' 'B,' and 'C' schools" (Murray and Howe, 2017, p. 7). Observers reach the conclusion that "the formulas by which school report cards are computed are often not readily available, and are inscrutably byzantine in any case" (Murray and Howe, 2017, p. 9).

Echo Leadership

In addition to the worthless, random, imprecise judgments rendered when policymakers and ideologues array standardized test results, sanctions exacerbate the negative impact on traditional public education already created by the indeterminate zone. Educators respond to the vandalism done by standardized testing with test-prep and knee-jerk pedagogy. School leaders are relegated to what amounts to *echo leadership*, a parroting of free market standards for teaching and learning, in hopes that repeating the mantra of free market standardization will yield success. Echo leadership is the fruitless response to the vandalism done to public education by what one renowned scholar refers to as *disruptors* (Ravitch, 2020).

Echo leadership illustrates a fundamental impediment to function of leadership: standardized accountability measures are unrelated to the original power of education. School leaders echo free market theory while accountability to students is abandoned.

Under these circumstances, learning is relegated to imprinting upon the echo transmitted by the so-called reforms in free market theory. Imprinting ensures that there is little impetus for the exchange of ideas in educational environments. Standardized accountability forces educators and students to become, at best, mimics of rudimentary, lock-step, lower-order teaching and learning. Echo leadership is nothing less than a response to:

> pressures [that] influence what teachers teach, marginalize low-stakes subjects, divert resources to students based on their likelihood of passing the test, and increase the time devoted to teaching test taking skills as distinct from the

content being tested. (Booher-Jennings, 2006; Diamond and Spillane, 2004; Firestone, Mayrowetz, and Fairman, 1998; Jacob, 2005; McNeil, 2002; Smith, 1998; Valenzuela, 2004; Wilson and Floden, 2001) (Spillane, Parise, and Zoltners Sherer, 2011, pp. 586–587).

Finding the Voice of Function of Leadership

The echoes that distort the "voice" of present-day educational leadership can be eliminated. Functional educational leadership eliminates echoes with "a combination of skills and traits [that] can help to explain why some leaders are able to recognize what pattern of behavior is relevant, how much of each behavior is optimal, and when to use the behaviors" (Yukl, 2012, p. 77). Instead of responding to distortions, instead of stumbling over marbles in the indeterminate zone, and instead of acquiescing to inadequate and unreliable options for leadership, intentional educational leaders can enact function.

PICTURING FUNCTIONAL EDUCATIONAL LEADERSHIP

Functional educational leaders understand that organizations are defined "as existing 'in the interrelationships between activities of individuals' (Hubbard, Mehan, and Stein, 2005, p. 263)" (Daly, 2009, p. 173). Interrelations between and among activities are multidirectional and reciprocal. Functional educational leadership is public work that is multidirectional and reciprocal on behalf of student agency for public life and citizenship participation in democracy as illustrated in figure 9.1.

> Because leadership is concerned with working with and through other people, it implies the need to build interpersonal capacity for leadership. This level of capacity is grounded in an assumption of reciprocal influence through expertise, reason, reputation, personality, and interpersonal skills (Mitchell and Sackney, 2001; Sackney and Mitchell, 2002, p. 907).

Function embodies the intentionality, reciprocity, and interconnectivity of educational leadership. The choice to enact function is among the most significant that any school leader can make.

In the Picture: The Systemic Ecology of Intentionality

Educators incorporate their life experience, prior learning, research base, context, and instructional function throughout their professional practice. From

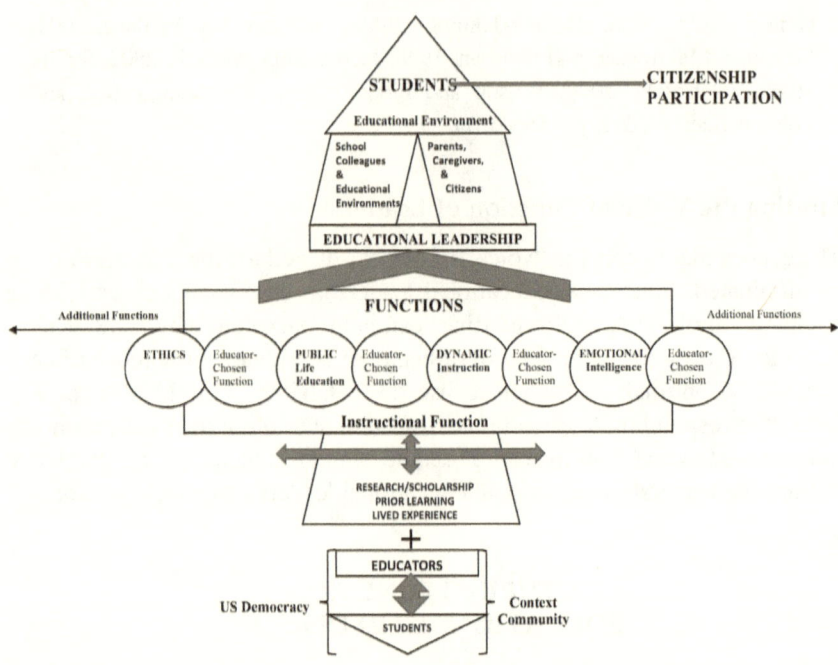

Figure 9.1 Functional Educational Leadership. *Source*: Author created.

this foundation, and with the understanding that this foundation is subject continuously to external and internal influences, functions interconnect and interact based on a leader's intentions (see figure 9.1).

As leaders intend, knowledge, skills, virtue, emotions, lived experience, research, and professional experiences become the baseline for professional practice. Intentionality underlies an educator's decisions and behaviors. From intentions, then, educators make choices that establish, implement, evaluate, and improve educational environments aligned with functions.

Scholars speak to the nature of these educational environments as *systemic* (Rice, 2017). Systemic educational environments are a host of interconnectivities. Functional leadership, the interconnectivities necessary to foster systemic habits of public creation, is the professional capability to enact educational environments as ecologies.

Within the ecology of a public school are biomes or micro-environments referred to with names like classroom, cafeteria, gym, hallway, and school bus. The interactions, socialization, and interconnectivity of educational biomes are subject—directly or indirectly—to the intentions of school leaders. Function chosen by leadership, or function ignored in leadership, determines whether US public education resembles the International Space Station (ISS) or a perilous plane flight.

FUNCTION AND THE CONSTRUCTION OF EDUCATIONAL LEADERSHIP

The challenges of educational leadership frequently tempt educators and others to observe that educational leadership is like *building the plane while it's flying*. This analogy conveys the difficulty and drama of day-to-day educational leadership but it ignores one vital fact: constructing a plane in the air would lead only to disaster.

Perhaps the disconnections engendered by the indeterminate zone or the ill-conceived mentality of "reform," or the frantic pace of day-to-day leadership prevent scholars and practitioners from reconsidering building-the-plane-aloft as a suitable analogy for educational leadership. Moreover, external and internal political perils, less than adequate funding, innumerable intrusive mandates, and ineffective practices can overwhelm leadership and how school leaders reflect upon the profession.

Forswearing these and other distractions, an analogy that better suits function of educational leadership is that it's like *sustaining the ISS*. On the ISS, additions and repairs occur in space without endangering the spacecraft, its mission, and the crew. By realizing this same degree of intention, interconnectivity, and continuous improvement, educational leadership sustains safe and purposive "flight" via function.

Enacting function, educational leaders step over the metaphorical threshold of ongoing practice and let go of the theories, ideologies, and practices that keep educational leadership grounded. The journey that lies ahead for educational leadership, at this point, becomes public work.

Functional Educational Leadership Is Public Work

Public work is the "prize" that commands the focus of functional educational leadership. Boyte (2011) defines public work as "self-organized efforts by a mix of people who solve common problems and create things, material or symbolic, of lasting civic value (pp. 632–633)" (Knight Abowitz, 2018, p. 8). Functional educational leadership is public work because it engages all students with the capacities necessary and sufficient for problem-solving and habits of public creation necessary and sufficient for both personal success and public life success that constitute things of lasting civic value for US democracy.

The civic value of functional educational leadership lies in this interweaving function to engage student capacities in the public work of mutuality, "I" and "we." Functions are enacted so that the original power of education engages all students with the capacities of fairness, positive liberty, respect, social justice, and humility. Public life education, then citizenship education, become habits of public creation under the aegis of functional educational leadership.

HOW TO FUNCTION AS AN EDUCATIONAL LEADER

Functional educational leadership is within the grasp of US public educators. As discussed earlier, agency is the intentional enactment of function fostered by commitment to professional decisions and behaviors that are instrumental, relational, and *both/and*. Agency, the "how" of functional educational leadership, evolves when educators:

- "Build interpersonal capacity by giving attention to, talking about, supporting, and rewarding collegiality, inquiry, collective reflection, and collaborative processes (Deal and Peterson, 1998)" (Sackney and Mitchell, 2002, p. 908).
- Nurture schools and their biomes based on the knowledge that "organizational capacity is significant because, without structures to bring people together and to engage them in school-wide processes, personal and interpersonal capacity for leadership remain disjointed, incoherent, and impotent" (Sackney and Mitchell, 2002, p. 908).
- Implement functions as an essential part of organizational capacity generated by school leaders who understand the nature of leadership as *"primus inter pares*—first among equals—taking us away from notions of leadership as hierarchy, which invokes not leadership, but mastery" (Ciulla et al., 2018, p. 9). Leadership is process by any staff member of stepping forward to take responsibility, to see other points of view, to make ethical judgments, to act and pay the cost of action (Ciulla et al., 2018).

Functional leadership intends interconnectivities. For example, functions (see figure 9.1) interconnect with foundation elements of individual character, emotion, and cognition within the strengths, lived experience, meaning-making, collective identity, I identify as . . . statements, and "we" of colleagues and students that flourish in educational environments that evince the original power of education.

Interconnectivities are manifest further in the poly-collegial commitment of functional educational leaders. This commitment relies upon and plays to each educator's strengths throughout interconnected foundational elements (e.g., prior learning, context, instructional function) that all colleagues bring to professional practice. This commitment also fosters the agency of principled reasoning via what Sackney and Mitchell (2002) refer to as *affirmation* and *invitation*.

"Affirmation means that people can disagree radically on a host of issues but still value and learn from other's opinions, ideas, or contributions" (Sackney and Mitchell, 2002, p. 904). Invitation is the deliberate including of every school colleague in the dialogues that speak to the creating of a good school on behalf of all students (Sackney and Mitchell, 2002). Shared, the intentions of functional educational leadership connect colleagues and students to the greater good.

Misperceptions of Function and Educational Leadership

If function does not develop in educational leadership during the remainder of the twenty-first century, two misperceptions may be responsible for such an outcome. The first of these misperceptions is the presumption that leadership is expressed by whatever the individual with a title thinks, does, or wants. The second of these is the presumption that school leadership is responsible for creating schooling that conforms to the adage that "the best thing that business can do for education, is to make education a business (Abrams, 2016)" (Rice, 2017, p. 56).

These misperceptions rest on the counterproductive understanding that educational leadership should take its cue from "a deficit model of human behavior. Scholars and practitioners have tended to focus on ways to correct problems and punish misbehaviors rather than to promote growth" (Murphy, Seashore Louis, and Smylie, 2017, p. 23). Punishment and correction, enforcement of the prerogatives of an efficient organization, are management characteristics that supersede function.

Adding to this collage of misperceptions, external accountability measures imposed by standardized testing and accountability-as-ideology "reduce local discretion, autonomy and creativity, narrow curriculum; and constrain teaching pedagogy (Toenjes, Dworkin, Gary, Jon, and Antwanett, 2000)" (Goldring and Greenfield, 2002, p. 10).

This assault on interconnectivity yields education as a static enterprise whose viability is determined by linear, one-variable, assessment. The educational environments crafted by present-day leadership are reduced to the linearity of "supply and value chains [where] inputs are measured, as are outputs and a single metric, profit (or share price), can be proffered as a comprehensive measure of business success" (Rice, 2017, p. 58).

In this static state schools and educational leadership are manipulated into objects or products by statute, reduced funding, and standardized accountability. These products subvert the original power of education, justify management, and rationalize "reform" of public schools.

But functional educational leadership is not a tool whose purpose is to sculpt change. Fraise and Brooks (2015) illuminate this point:

We partially reject the notion that culture can be sharped to suit administrative purposes and suggest that schools and communities, considered as a whole, are more properly characterized as a protean constellation of individuals and groups to be understood and respected for what they can teach and learn rather than as some malleable substance that can (and should) be changed. (p. 8)

Enacting functional educational leadership is a commitment to all students. Beginning with this intention, educators have the foundational elements from which instructional function emerges to foster multidimensional and reciprocal functions enacted by school leadership in educational environments that engage all students with the original power of education en route to citizenship participation in US democracy.

LOOKING AT THIS CHAPTER IN THE REARVIEW MIRROR

Enacting function depends upon the intentionality of educational leadership. This is a difficult but necessary choice if the original power of education and the moral obligation of public education are to establish the teaching and learning that all US students deserve during the remainder of the twenty-first century.

Several questions bring together ideas presented in this chapter and ask readers to reflect upon educational leadership, enacting function, and the need for a transformation of how school leaders construct their professional practice:

- What role do *affirmation* and *invitation* play in the enactment of function? Can these elements of functional educational leadership play a role in how school leaders understand their role?
- Summarize functional educational leadership using figure 9.1. What do leaders in your school or school district need to include in a similar illustration to bring leadership and functions together?
- In your own words, define educational leadership. In your own words, describe how leadership is enacted, how it occurs, in your school or school district in alignment with your definition of educational leadership. How is what you've defined and described different from or similar to how functional educational leadership is portrayed in this chapter?
- Should educational leadership be "public work" as this concept is shared in this chapter? Defend your answer with evidence from your own professional experiences and from the ideas shared in this chapter.

Chapter 10

Details, Details, Details

The devil, they say, is in the details. On the one hand, details facilitate organizing, resourcing, monitoring, boundary-spanning, problem-framing, communicating, modeling, and making-meaning/sense (Murphy et al., 2016, p. 459). Details are the grease for the activities of function. On the other hand, unattended or misunderstood details are often the root of leadership dysfunction. If leaders are not detail-oriented, the good school, comprehensive public education, and student-centric educational environments can be compromised. If leaders micro-manage, they fixate on details to the exclusion of a greater educational good.

A music professor, a friend of one of the authors, put this another way, "The difference between excellence and average is details" (Guy, Todd, Personal communication, 1998). To shed light on detail-oriented leadership, this chapter discusses:

- Signals and messages in the details.
- Leadership of details: Anticipation and assessment.
- Inquiring, surveying, and gardening for signals.
- Leadership as signaling.
- The indignity in the details.

DETAILS SEND SIGNALS AND SIGNALS ARE MESSAGES

Among the most important signals and messages relevant to leadership are the details that comprise the "atmosphere" of an organization. How a leader processes and responds to details, the signals they send, and the messages in the signals can be the difference between excellence and average, or, between average and awful.

Leaders' engagement with details can maximize or complicate the intentionality of leadership. Detail averse leadership interrupts interconnectivities among the rungs of the double helix. Ignored, unattended, or mishandled, details can invoke significant dysfunction.

Leadership of Details: Anticipation and Assessment

The time-honored epigram about the devil-in-the-details is itself a signal about the importance of organizational minutia. The message that this well-known phrase sends is significant: leaders can have a devil of a time understanding details and what to do about their signals and messages. This message suggests that making sense out of details is an always-there task for leadership.

Anticipation of Details

Anticipation is one aspect of the task that details represent for leaders. Leaders who anticipate details (e.g., calendaring and preparation-in-advance for regular events, obligations, and deadlines; delegating and incorporating follow-up reminders to designees; reviewing notes and files from the most recent event, obligation, or deadline) put themselves and their organizations in position to maximize the coherence of interconnectivities among functions.

Some details (encountered by administrative interns while working on site with school leaders) suggest the scope and value of anticipation: evaluating instruction, creating consensus in a group, ensuring effective lesson design, putting research-based practices to work, reflecting on a professional dilemma or completed task, and gathering information about recently promulgated policy (Lehman, 2013, pp. 130–131).

Thinking ahead about details engages a leader in anticipating messages and their consequences including how school context or circumstances might affect decisions, plans, or activities; how external factors (e.g., state mandates, community concerns, societal problems) might facilitate or obstruct the primary purpose of public education, or how interactions among colleagues and students might permit moving forward with dynamic instruction and effective evaluation (Swensson and Shaffer, 2020).

Assessment of Details

Leaders must assess the meaning in messages and the relevance of these messages to the primary purpose and moral obligation of US public education. The detail-oriented school leader, for example, analyzes the signals and messages "sent" by her/his choices about details that affect teaching and learning.

Sizing up the impact of details and whether details enhance the reliability of leadership. For instance, Goldring et al. (2007) proffer a framework to assess the details of *learning-centered leadership*. A leader's self-assessment of details associated with learning-centered leadership looks for "the intersection of *what* principals or leadership teams must accomplish to improve academic and social learning for all students (the core components) and *how* they create those core components (the key processes)" (Goldring et al., 2007, p. 18).

TRUST IS A DETAIL

A detail that no leader can ignore is trust. The value of trust in classrooms, schools, and school districts is affirmed by several observers (Balyer, 2017; Mitchell, Kensler, and Tschannen-Moran, 2016 in Press; Swensson and Shaffer, 2020; Van Wart, 2013; Wahlstrom and Seashore Louis, 2008). In the absence of trust, the good public school, educational adequacy, and the original power of teaching and learning are lost "'[because] people divert their energy into self-protection and away from learning' (Mitchell and Sackney, 2000, p. 49)" (Sackney and Mitchell, 2002, p. 902).

Caring to ask colleagues about their families, their well-being, their plans for vacation/holiday, or their hobbies is attention to detail that brings emotional intelligence into professional daily interactions and that builds trust. Attributes in everyday conversation with colleagues and caring responses to details shared in these attributes are the building blocks of trust.

Sackney and Mitchell (2002) illustrate that "trust has three dimensions: trust between individuals, trust between the individual and the organization, and trust in events and processes" (p. 902). Ethics as a function of leadership supports all three dimensions.

With the understanding that trust is built over time and that trust is a gift that not all are able or willing to share, school leaders have an obligation to every colleague to be trustworthy. Being trustworthy is a composite of behaviors chosen by leaders that are honest, straightforward, others-serving, and ethical (Van Wart, 2013). These behaviors and the values assigned to them by others are engaged by a leader's principled reasoning, caring, and justice.

DETAIL-ORIENTED LEADERSHIP

Detail-oriented leadership (e.g., anticipation, assessment, informal, and formalized practices) is like sonar. Leaders send questions, observations, and choices into the organizational ecology. These questions, observations, and choices generate "returns." These returns suggest the shape of details. Leaders are responsible for making sense of these "returns" and for making sense of the formal or informal practices that best respond. To make the most of "returns," leaders inquire, survey, and garden.

Inquiring for "Returns"

Taking a cue from the investment in inquiry made in all classrooms, school leaders put questions to work to induce "returns." Although written surveys or online questions can help gather feedback about details, inquiry that occurs informally immerses leaders in a range of details. The impact of dialogue and interaction demonstrates the value of informal inquiry and suggests Senge's (1990) observation that dialogue contributes to the development of a learning organization.

Leaders who make a point every day to be present in hallways, classrooms, and cafeterias (both student and adult dining areas) create dynamic opportunities for "returns." Inquiring for returns depends upon and continuously improves trust. To this end, the purpose for inquiring-while-walking-about must be clear. When the purpose for an inquiry is shared, leaders should indicate if/how results will be shared and what action, if any, will be taken in response to the results. "Returns" from informal inquiry can be transformative when questions like these perform like sonar:

- What's the process or procedure that we use in our school that helps you the most?
- What's the process or procedure that we use in our school that is the least helpful to you and that needs substantial improvement? What do you suggest we do to make the necessary improvements?
- Is there a detail or procedure in our school that we should be paying attention to but, right now, we're not?
- Among our colleagues, who has the best ideas about details or procedures that make a positive difference for student learning?
- What's the detail or procedure in your daily work that concerns you the most and what might I do to ease this concern?
- How did another school or school district where you worked handle a detail or procedure that we could use to make ourselves more effective?

Surveying for "Returns"

Surveying offers a unique precision to leaders as they encounter and evaluate signals. Surveying is formal leadership behavior that seeks returns.

Deliberately gathering signals and messages is another way to engage in attention to detail that leads to reflection, decision-making, and action. Surveying seeks "returns" from details that are non-negotiables:

- *Safety:* Are all exterior doors closed and locked throughout the school day? Are all classrooms equipped with an emergency "safety-go bag"? Do all colleagues know how to alert the whole school if any developing situation requires a lockdown? Are all fire alarms and fire extinguishers in working order? Are safety procedures reviewed with all staff at the start of each school year and are these procedures updated regularly with input from local first responders and other relevant authorities? Are all colleagues knowledgeable about reporting requirements if any student is suspected to be a victim of child abuse?
- *First impressions:* Are entry doors and vestibules swept or vacuumed every day immediately after students arrive? Are hallways swept or "matted" on a regular schedule during each school day? Is signage clear and up-to-date throughout the school?
- *Cleanliness:* Are restrooms clean and stocked with soap, toweling, toilet paper, and other necessities? Are restrooms checked for these details on a daily schedule? Are cafeteria tables cleaned before each different lunch period? Are sufficient trash containers available during lunch and is trash removed regularly during lunch periods? Is the serving line and serving area clean throughout lunch? Are colleagues on the food service team trained regularly for safe food service, proper food storage, and safe operation of equipment? Is the custodial team trained to clean classrooms effectively, respond to emergency situations, and to deal with hazardous waste?
- *Large-scale maintenance:* Does the school district perform preventative maintenance on major building systems annually? Does the school district replace/upgrade major building systems (e.g., HVAC, roof, plumbing, electrical, flooring) after so many years? Are there procedures in place to ensure that major building systems function effectively and safely during school holidays and other long-term breaks?
- *Mandated reports and compliance issues:* Are there clear "pathways" for completing reports mandated by the central office, the state, and/or the federal government? Are colleagues trained to comply with the requirements that pertain to students with special needs? Are parents/caregivers and school guests informed (in advance where possible) about the ID requirements for visiting school? Are all safety mandates and reporting requirements fulfilled? Are all colleagues updated each year about expectations for the administration of standardized assessments?
- *Our "people business":* Are formal practices in place to help any student who becomes ill or is hurt while at school? Are processes in place for

helping any colleague who becomes ill at school or who receives emergency news about a family crisis? Are procedures in place that allow any colleague to alert leaders about family or relationship crises that have the potential to affect the school community? Is there a caring and emotionally intelligent culture throughout the school modeled by all school leaders?

Gardening for "Returns"

Gardening is about paying attention to details, small and large, to ensure that a healthy verdant garden is the result. Gardening by educational leaders anticipates and assesses details found in activities and agency such as:

- *Monitoring Delegation:* Delegation, engaging the strengths of professional colleagues to accomplish tasks, recognizes the leadership capacities of all professional educators. Engaging colleagues with assignments that access their leadership strengths or that grow new professional capacities is a response to detail often referred to as collaboration. As important as it is for leaders to delegate, it's equally important to monitor and support the work of the colleagues to whom a task has been delegated. Leaders often garden this detail by using a "delegation calendar" on which is written the task delegated, the person to whom it's delegated, and the "due date" for task completion. On the calendar, between the date of assignment and the "due date" appointments help monitor and support the delegation.
- *Creating Feedback:* Ask colleagues about specific programs, objectives, problems, or other issues. Make time to create feedback. Then, listen. While listening, leaders garden actively by paraphrasing what's being said and asking if the paraphrase is accurate from the colleague's point of view. Later, within a week, provide feedback to the person(s) you talked with about the issue/idea that you paraphrased.
- *Encouraging Growth:* When building-level staff development occurs, gardening engages colleagues in strategies or practices for which they will be responsible:
  - *Paraphrase sheets:* Every staff development participant writes an anonymous paraphrase of the idea shared during staff development and how they are going to enact what's been presented. Reading these anonymous summaries will allow leaders to make decisions about maximizing use of the idea.
  - *Get 'er Done Day/Week:* Designate a day, week, or some other appropriate timeframe during which colleagues are to "get done" the strategy, program, or other practice presented during staff development. Visual evidence of the enactment of the strategy, program, or practice is to be created and made available in each classroom.

- *Call & Response Visits:* During a faculty meeting or some other designated after-school meeting, colleagues visit classrooms to view the get 'er done evidence. Colleagues carry sticky notes with them and post comments or questions beside the evidence.
  - *Back at the meeting:* When colleagues return to the original meeting, verbal comments in praise of the way that evidence was shared and in praise of the student work that demonstrated the impact of the evidence are shared.
- *Giving Away the "Office Anchor":* The tendency to think that staying in the office is the best way to garden and anchor yourself to the details of the job is more an albatross than a stabilizing force. Make a point every day to walk through the building, classrooms, and cafeteria if you're a building leader and make a point to schedule in-the-buildings hours during every week if you're a school district leader.
- *Listening to Experience:* At times the most important detail and the most urgent message are a leader's experience. Experience is sometimes referred to as an educator's intuition or *that little voice that says "do something."* Experience can be an accumulation of or accounting for numerous, apparently unrelated, details that represent the proverbial *voice of experience.* Often, such informal, spontaneous, out-of-the-blue, assessments rendered by experience are of immense value.

Indignity Can Be in the Details

America's students deserve educators who are attentive and responsive to details. Functional educational leadership cannot be ethical and it cannot create educational environments that fulfill the moral obligation of public education without confronting ideological and societal forces that visit devastating details upon our students and our democracy.

The damage done by the details in ideology and legislation afflict public education in the twenty-first century. Data collected in the early part of the second decade of the twenty-first century, for example, demonstrates that "43 percent of the nation's private school students attended virtually all-white schools" (Suitts, 2019). The duty of public educators to confront these details is illustrated by data that indicates that "by 2013, more than 50 percent of the nation's public schoolchildren were from low-income families and almost half were children of color" (Suitts, 2019).

Ironically, these details are buried beneath the allegation that "the public school is a socialized or politically monopolized institution and suffers from weakness inherent in all monopolies" (Suitts, 2019). This allegation, and others like it, that public education constitutes an assault on individual freedom is a message sent by details that functional educational leadership must confront.

The indignity in messages like this is magnified when educators, policymakers, and civic leaders do not enact functions including emotional intelligence and ethics. Failure to act on messages is not only ghost leadership but also the harbinger of ongoing indignities. For example, Georgia's voters gave voice to the message of fear and racism when they approved an amendment to the state's constitution which stated, "freedom from compulsory association at all levels of public education shall be preserved inviolate" (Suitts, 2019).

ATTENTION TO DETAIL: A LEADER'S MESSAGE

Educators monitor and adjust. Monitoring, teaching, leading, thinking, speaking, and learning give educators abilities to adjust on-the-fly to the messages in details. Because functional educational leadership is intentional, monitoring, adjusting, and reflecting are essential attributes of professional self-mastery. Attention to detail, then, is not only a signal sent by leaders but it is a message that leaders send to themselves from questions such as:

- How do students experience dynamic instruction and how do I help improve this?
- How do colleagues express and demonstrate caring in our environments? Who do I enlist to coach more integration of dynamic instruction and caring?
- What are the ethical strengths of our school that have the greatest positive impact on students?
- Do colleagues throughout our school have suggestions about improving the emotional intelligence of our services and our interactions with our students, their parents/caregivers, and the community? To enact improvements, are there allies in the community and/or advocates among colleagues whose input and agency can move all of us forward?
- Why are the rungs within my functional educational leadership successful and what should I do to strengthen and improve existing rungs while paying attention to signals that imply less than reliable functioning in my leadership?
- Can community be fostered more completely throughout the educational environments within the school or school district? Whose wisdom and talent should be accessed to inquire about community? What should I do as a leader to augment and expand the way community intertwines with the other rungs throughout the double helix of my leadership?

Leading is a message about its own details. Leading is a detail in an organization in the sense that all who are engaged with or affected by the organization pay attention to the details that are leadership. Principals, for example, hold many levers that can assist and inform leadership practices, even and especially those enacted by the community of leaders. At the very least, the school principal can serve as a model, a facilitator, a learner, and a questioner (Mitchell and Sackney, 2000) for it is through observation and questions that people arrive at inquiry and reflection. (Sackney and Mitchell, 2002, p. 909)

So Many Detail-Oriented Observers

Leaders are not alone as they attend to the details about their professional practice and individual behavior. At school and outside of school, so many colleagues, students, parents/caregivers, and citizens are also detail-oriented. Details about a leader and the messages they send (intentionally or unintentionally) are thoroughly scrutinized. What people observe about a leader's attention to detail affects the organization and the pursuit of its primary purpose.

LOOKING AT THIS CHAPTER IN
THE REARVIEW MIRROR

Educational leaders are surrounded by details. Several questions shared here give readers the opportunity to summarize this chapter and to orient their own engagement with details and the atmosphere in their school:

- Are there formalized practices that impose or exacerbate indignities in your educational environments and, if there are, what response is appropriate to ensure that details do not inhibit the teaching and learning that all students deserve?
- Among the many inquiries about details posed in this chapter, which are NOT attended to well in your school and how can this situation be improved?
- What are the questions about details that were not asked in this chapter that you would add to ensure that leadership functions effectively?
- Which leadership behaviors dealt with in this chapter should you improve in your own practice and what details in your own professionalism will you attend to so that observable improvement is created and sustained?

Chapter 11

Reliable Educational Leadership

Reliability is the extent or degree to which an assessment or specification can be relied upon to be accurate. In education, *reliability* is a term most often relegated to discussions about standardized testing. But reliability is a concept whose merit extends well beyond testing.

Reliability, however, is rarely part of the conversation about educational leadership. This is the case for several reasons. First, like the movie *Groundhog Day*, teaching and learning in US public schools are trapped in an endless and counterproductive scenario. In the case of public education, standardized testing yields unreliable results with no connection with how to think, and this leads to more testing that initiates an unending repetition of this sequence.

Compounding this damage, educational leadership and public educators are judged by test results so that a fruitless pursuit of standardized expectations is reinforced.

Next, society's expectations about good public schools have mutated. Expectations for better test results disconnect student capacities from teaching and learning associated with the original power of education. Finally, because public educators are impelled to respond to these expectations, leadership, educational environments, and achievement results are inherently unreliable.

To escape the expectation of unreliability, public educators owe students a mutually consistent and intentional effort to construct and interconnect functions that can be depended upon to engage learners with the original power of education. Reliability, it turns out, is within the grasp of US educators. Reliability depends, however, on ending inaccurate and undependable practices that impose Groundhog Day on public education.

This state of affairs afflicts public education, in part, because leaders, educators, and schools have attended to mandates that "are about what we know, not what we should know" (English, 2005, p. 82). In this chapter, the proposition is advanced that reliability is the *should be* of expectations for educational leadership and US public education. Reliable educational leadership cannot develop unless educational leadership is reimagined.

This chapter examines a future in which school leadership relies on function to establish accurately the educational environments that all students deserve. This future reimagines the expectations for educational leadership. Consideration of reliable educational leadership is encouraged via dialogue about these questions:

- Can educational leadership be reliable?
- What *should* we expect from US public education?
- What are the expectations of function?
- What *is* expected of public education?
- Are reliability and educational function compatible?

THE ECOLOGY OF RELIABLE EDUCATIONAL LEADERSHIP

Reliable educational leadership is not perfect leadership. Rather, reliable leadership maximizes the extent to which educational environments can be depended upon for accurate enactment of the original power of education on behalf of all students.

Leithwood (1999) invoked reliability as a significant topic across the realm of public education in his discussion about *highly reliable organizations*. Greenfield (2004) synopsized reliable schools as "schools which more consistently and reliably accomplish that which we expect of schools" (p. 183). What is expected of schools and how these expectations are manifest give voice to reliable school leadership.

What *Should Be* the Expectations for US Public Education?

Discarded expectations are strewn about the beleaguered realm of American public education. Relationships hypothesized between public education and a greater good, the principles of democracy, and meaningful learning for all students are curtailed. Under assault by the forces of privatization (Ravitch, 2020) and standardized accountability (Swensson and Shaffer, 2020), present-day public education is impelled to fulfill expectations that have little to do with the original power of education, mutuality, democracy, or social justice.

The Expectation of Virtue

Wayward imperatives so overwhelm educational leadership that reliability is rarely expected from public education. But reimagining the expectation of reliability is within the capabilities and capacities of public educators if virtue jump-starts America's expectation for educational leadership.

Virtue is the expectation at the foundation of mutually consistent interactions in educational leadership. Discussed earlier, virtue is "an excellence that encompasses both ethics and competency" (Ciulla et al., 2018, p. 5). Leadership can determine in advance where it is expected to go on behalf of all students when it relies upon virtue to determine and reach the destination. The relationship between ethics and competency is a gyroscope that enables school leaders to reflect upon agency necessary and sufficient to enact reliability intentionally.

Ethics are "deeply rooted in responsibility involving imagination and ability to see other viewpoints; willingness to judge for oneself; and willingness to act, and to pay for these actions, if need be" (Ciulla et al., 2018, p. 9). Competencies (e.g., principled reasoning, positive liberty, justice of caring, complex pedagogies) put educational leaders in position to engage all students with the original power of education.

From Virtue: The Expectation of Reliability

The raison d'etre of US public education is the pursuit of a greater good, an egalitarian society, and a principled democracy. When this reason for being underlies educational leadership, the wellspring of reliable leadership, virtue, incorporates several expectations that *should be* driving US public education:

- *US citizenship participation is socially just.* The theoretical principles interwoven across documents at the foundation of US democracy espouse social justice. The right of every citizen to the same opportunities unfettered by prejudice, illegality, or marginalization depends upon the participation of every citizen in US democracy. This expectation means that singularity is abandoned in favor of mutuality and that mutuality is nurtured through the intentions of educational leadership that foster learning experiences for public life that engage students with capacities for citizenship participation that are socially just.
- *The primary purpose and moral obligation of American public education focus on the capacities for futures that all students deserve.* The conjunction of primary purpose and moral obligation in US public education is the expectation that educational leadership will enact educational environments that engage all students with the capacities necessary and sufficient for success in school, life, and citizenship.

- *Public education prepares all students for adaptive challenges.* Douglass (2018) calls attention to *adaptive challenges* which "are problems for which there is not an existing or predefined solution" (p. 388). The expectation that public education *leads-out* meaning-making and natural thinking of all students is the expectation that educational environments endowed with dynamic instruction engage learners with habits of mind and the values of the moral obligation of public education to develop the capacities of all students to meet adaptive challenges.
- *Public education serves the greater good of citizenship participation anchored by the principles of democracy, the social contract, positive liberty, principled reasoning, and the balance of social intelligence.* While student experiences with public life atrophy, this expectation of leadership in public education takes on expanded significance. Public education and the greater good are linked only if school leaders intentionally interconnect ethics, public life education, and dynamic instruction throughout the ecology of education.

Ecology of Leadership

A list of expectations, of course, is not reliable educational leadership. Instead, reliable educational leadership develops from an understanding of and an investment in the ecology of school leadership.

Darling's (2007) overview of ecological systems theory—"a theory of human development in which everything is seen as interrelated and our knowledge of development is bounded by context, culture, and history" (p. 204)—encapsulates an expectation that educational leadership should be an ecology. This ecology entails intentionality, interconnectivities, and instructional function as the means of reliable educational leadership.

The ecology of leadership fosters reliability in multiple and dynamic interconnectivities. School leadership develops educational environments throughout an ecology of interconnected expectations for virtue, mutuality, and the original power of education.

RELIABILITY AND THE ECOLOGY OF EDUCATIONAL ENVIRONMENTS

Baseball great Yogi Berra got it right. Educational leadership can't arrive at a reliable destination if that destination and how to reach it are left to whim, chance, or ignorance. Because educational leadership has in mind, at best, an indeterminate destination, leaders cannot be depended upon to enact accurately the educational environments that all US students deserve. Finding itself in the land of unreliability, educational leadership is exactly nowhere, just as baseball's preeminent philosopher predicted.

Ecological Principles for Reliable Leadership

A signal that reliable educational leadership requires agency to guide the interdependencies of an ecology is found in the observation by Wielkiewicz and Stelzner (2005) that "any attempt to understand the complexities of an organization by focusing on its leader is incomplete" (p. 326). Ecologies, instead, are interdependencies among processes and systems within organizations. Interdependence and interconnectivity symbolize the ecology of leadership. The ecology of leadership incorporates, but is not limited to, the myriad professional relationships within a school; the teaching and learning in the exchange that fuels the original power of education; and the reflection, self-correction, and self-efficacy of intentionality.

From these expectations for the ecology of leadership, reliability is fostered when educational leaders employ principled reasoning to enact function that establishes educational environments in which open systems suffused with internal and external feedback loops flourish. This ecology of leadership fosters and supports the ecology of educational environments. The agency of educational leadership responds to and nurtures these ecological characteristics to express and engage with patterns across functions to construct reliability.

The Process of Reliable Leadership

As this discussion illustrates, educational leadership is disconnected, for a variety of reasons, from reliability. Moreover, US public education is detached from the activities natural to it. School leaders, in response, rivet their professional practices to activities that divert public education from the original power of education. Spiraling away from reliability, teaching, learning, and leading sustain the malign forces and factors that dictate singularity, knee-jerk pedagogy, stereotype threat, ineffective assessment, and deficit-thinking.

Ending the disconnections and reversing the downward spiral are responsibilities that educational leadership must accept on behalf of the public education that all US students deserve. Interaction, after all, lies at the heart of virtue; ethics and competencies affect and are affected by each other.

By understanding *process*, the term used "to describe how leaders influence because the word implies an interaction; that is, leaders 'affect and are affected by' those they lead" (Abrahams, 2007, p. 87), school leaders initiate acceptance of the responsibility for coherence and reliability to reverse the downward spiral. Process is the capacity to "flatten organizations, provide more organic structures, enhance social integration, [and] create learning organizations" (Van Wart, 2013, p. 559).

Reliable leadership enacts accurately expectations that all students engage with the original power of education. This agency embodies the expectation that school professionals work "in ways that demonstrate the causal connection between their actions and what students learn" (Elmore, 2005, p. 141).

These expectations foster self-efficacy, professional courage, and action necessary to abandon lagging indicators and the other disconnections in *outcome accountability* to accomplish *process accountability*. "Process accountability means having to justify the *process* of making a decision" (Wielkiewicz and Stelzner, 2005, p. 333). Functional educational leadership is the ecology in which ongoing justification of decision-making evolves through reflection about *the good*, positive liberty, and mutuality.

THE "VOICE" OF RELIABILITY

In the indeterminate zone, under the thrall of intrusive mandates, and in the grasp of malign characteristics embedded in America's history, present-day educational leadership can be depended upon to struggle to engage all students with reliable educational environments. Expected to "make do," school leaders are frequently condemned to unreliability.

Present-day expectations prompt unreliability in public education and its leadership. The extent to which these expectations can be depended upon to be accurate specifications for the success of all students is dubious. Mountains of research, for example, indicate that present-day expectations for student achievement are unreliable (Swensson, Ellis, and Shaffer, 2019a, b). Present-day expectations do little to facilitate the engagement of all US students with the original power of education and the outcomes intended by instructional function (see figures 5.2 and 9.1).

Reliability is about expectations. In the gap between what ought to be expected of US public education and what is expected in present-day public education, lies the opportunity for reliable leadership of US public education.

To make a difference, educational leadership cannot be about a singular "vision" but, instead, must be about "voice" (Sackney and Mitchell, 2002). The mission of leaders is one in which "the ascendancy of voice affirms the presence of multiple visions and diverse cultural meanings; it encourages participation, empowerment, collegiality, and consensus management; and it promotes a democratic culture of inquiry and discourse" (Sackney and Mitchell, 2002, p. 900). Educational leaders speak to reliability when they function as an *active person.*

The Active Person and Reliable Leadership

The applicability of this discussion to day-to-day practice of reliable public school leadership is related to key domains of Bronfenbrenner's ecological systems theory. Specifically, *active person* shapes ecologies. Educational leadership becomes active person for the ecologies of educational environments.

Greenfield (2004) offers a transformative question—"What ought I to *do*?" (p. 178)—that invokes educational leadership as *active person* of development for reliability throughout educational environments:

- The active person is intentional.
- Instructional function is development of and by every active person/educator. As shown in figure 5.1, the baseline of the ecology of functional educational leadership is instructional function. All educators develop instructional function. All educators are developed by their own instructional function and the instructional functions developing throughout the ecology of schools and school districts. What an educator *does* is inseparable from teaching, and teaching is inseparable from instructional function. What the active person ought to *do* hinges on the relationship each educator constructs between virtue and instructional function.
- The active person builds functional educational leadership by employing the cognitive, emotional, and behavioral capacities for self-mastery (balance and reciprocity), mutuality, respect, and efficacy.
- The end-in-mind and the eye on the prize allow the active person to focus function on "the essential human character of school organizations, their educative purpose, and the moral nature of the administrator's task" (Greenfield, 2004, p. 181).
- Opportunity and challenge in the ecologies of public schools are determinate if educational leaders intend that their habits of public creation construct the *should be* expectations that undergird functional educational leadership.

SPEAKING TO HIGHLY RELIABLE EDUCATIONAL LEADERSHIP

Highly reliable educational leadership (HREL) is development of a public thing by the active person that evokes the original power of education throughout educational environments for all students. Intentionality of HREL is agency that takes account of:

- The observation by Knight Abowitz and Stitzlein (2018) that public schools "can create the conditions for an educated citizenry with the knowledge and capacity for working with diverse others in negotiating our common fate together" (p. 37).
- Charisma is a dead-end for leadership and just as the free market for schooling disdains public life and social justice, the moral obligation of public education is a benchmark that cannot develop from singularity of leadership. Instead, as Ladson-Billings (2006) indicates "in democratic nations, that personal responsibility must be coupled with social responsibility" (p. 8).
- Hallinger and Heck (2002) put voice and organizational mission among these attributes as a symbiotic relationship. "An organizational mission exists when the personal visions of a critical mass of people cohere in a common sense of purpose within a community" (p. 12).

Although none of this striving is perfect—the authors are baseball fans and acknowledge the wisdom behind *you can't bat a thousand*, a phrase that acknowledges that no one gets a hit every time at bat—the expectations that public education must meet for all students suggest the intention of *HREL* to enact function reliably on behalf of all students.

When school leaders intend *HREL*, expectations for US public education during the remainder of the twenty-first century include:

- Taking responsibility for teaching and learning that "'communicates to students the school's attitudes toward a range of issues and problems, including how the school views them as human beings' (Beachum and McCray, 2011, p. 3)" (Fraise and Brooks, 2015, p. 11). Function of school leadership, in this way, evokes student capacities to wonder, inquire, encounter, accommodate, research, and dissent about what *should be known* and what *should be done* in a democratic society.
- Enacting functions of educational leadership for "the transformation of shared vision into reality, with an emphasis on cooperation (vs. competition), incorporating Indigenous ways of knowing or cultural intuition and rational thinking in problem solving, where power and influence are shared within a group" (Santamaria and Santamaria, 2015, p. 25).
- Seeking "to build bridges and cross borders so that the multiple cultures in the school-community can have empathy and define their own values instead of having this done by someone else" (Fraise and Brooks, 2015, p. 8).

WHAT *ARE* THE EXPECTATIONS FOR US PUBLIC EDUCATION?

Ecologically sound educational environments, much less the reliability of functional educational leadership, are not expectations throughout present-day US public education. Countervailing expectations have overtaken the relationship between US public education and the public good:

- *Have we changed yet?* The scholarly literature about educational leadership emphasizes the role that leaders play in changing their organization (Fernandez, 2005). An obsession with change, however, derails the imperative for coherence of purpose *while* improving a school or school district. Change implies the elimination, abandonment, or reversal of current trends, practices, or theories because they are worthless or wrong. Without prioritizing which trends, practices, or theories must be sustained, must be improved, or must change, leadership falls into a frenzy for change instead of a frenzy for enacting function of leadership for the educational environments that all students deserve. Furthermore, scholars observe "that the entire notion of reform in education may be the essence of the problem; that education cannot be reformed by a galvanizing strategy but rather, more likely, it can simply be improved (Tanner, 2013)" (Rice, 2017, p. 58). Perseverating on change and "reform" is the installation of unreliability.
- *Education is singularity.* Singularity is the oxymoronic expectation for all in present-day US public education. Singularity isolates and excludes when public education is in thrall to the ideology that spawns free market thinking. Singularity is the expectation of privatization that the needs of individuals outweigh the greater good. This expectation is a self-fulfilling prophecy: poor and minority cohorts of American students are not supposed to succeed academically but wealthy majority cohorts are. The expectation that marginalization and exclusion of any student or cohort of students is an inevitable part of education is the morally bankrupt premise embraced by too many policymakers, ideologues, and so-called leaders.
- *Education has a relationship with jobs.* The expectation that teaching and learning exist as a filtering mechanism to sort students into the job market obliterates the need to engage students with public life and citizenship education (Swensson and Shaffer, 2020). This expectation subverts the premise that public education exists to *lead-out* capacities and capabilities of all students. Preparing students for present-day jobs is the expectation of public education that denies a future where all students apply capabilities engendered by reliable educational environments to meet the inevitable unknowns in public life, economies, and personal fulfillment.
- *Unreliable from the very start.* Present-day leadership practice emphasizes unreliability. Standardized evaluation, from which public school leadership cannot escape, is expressed in "data on lagging outcomes (i.e., student achievement) [that] is generally used to inform and leverage changes in teacher practice, but without actually measuring the practices in which teachers engage" (Park et al., 2013). This enduring and damaging disconnection between how what is taught and measurement that highlights

undependable, inaccurate, outcomes divorced from teaching and learning is the unreliability that infests leadership and public education at its core.

WHAT ARE THE EXPECTATIONS OF FUNCTION?

The principles—projections or hopes within purpose—that underlie the expectations of US public education exist in the dedication and professional practice of millions of public educators throughout the United States. Each educator, each school, each school district strives to express these principles in the educational experiences of all students.

This embrace of function of leadership, of the public good instead of individual good, and of "voice" as mutuality throughout teaching and learning pursues the expectations that *should be* at the core of public education. What should be known about reliable educational leadership cannot emerge unless the expectations of function are fulfilled.

From this baseline, reliability develops via function of leadership. Function is the process in leadership of and for the ecology where relational, reciprocal, *active person*, and dialectical interconnectivities suffuse educational environments. Because virtue is the foundation of intentionality, functional educational leadership enacts the ecology of what *should be* for the capacities and lives of all US students.

In this way, school leaders undertake public work and in this way the construction of the intersection between how to think and the values of the moral obligation of public education fosters public life capabilities that undergird principles of and participation in US democracy.

Assessment of the confluence of dynamic instruction, ethics, and public life education, for instance, can affect and sustain the ecology of educational environments festooned with thinking skills like "listening, weighing evidence, communicating with people from diverse backgrounds, and thinking critically about, rather than merely accordance with, authority (Moses and Rogers, 2013, pp. 207–216)" (Murray and Howe, 2017, p. 13). The reliability of public education is nurtured via the ecological stewardship of functional educational leadership.

LOOKING AT THIS CHAPTER IN
THE REARVIEW MIRROR

The greatest difference that public educators can make is through a laser-like focus on what all students deserve from educational environments. Intentional choices made through the interconnectivity of functions are opportunities that educational leaders must grasp to serve all students and to improve their educational experiences.

Making a difference, thus, depends on "the level of conformity among educators' conceptions of responsibility, the organization's collective purposes, and the degree to which educators believe they influence or exercise agency over student learning" (Elmore, 2005, p. 137). The intentionality, justification, and self-efficacy of difference-making attends to the lived experience of all students. To make a difference, all public educators owe students an embrace of the increasing diversity of lived experience throughout America's student enrollment.

Elmore (2005) illustrates that present-day accountability constitutes a forced choice for school leaders. Either school leaders envelop teaching and learning to conform to the dictates of external accountability or educational leadership takes responsibility for locally sourced decision-making of internal accountability (Swensson and Shaffer, 2020). Self-efficacy is a difference-maker that educators must nurture and express persistently.

An ecological sense of educational leadership, and the influence of function to enact expectations for teaching and learning that *ought to be* synonymous with school leadership, are integrated throughout the panorama shared in this chapter. Within this chapter is an unwritten question upon which the future of reliable educational leadership turns: To function or not to function? If public educators are to confront the factors that render America's schools unreliable, function becomes the "how" of a reimagined educational leadership.

Making this commitment, educational leadership across America's public schools must recognize the tenacity, patience, and hard work required. Fortunately, these attributes are neither newly acquired nor unusual characteristics of public educators.

The following statements and questions are intended to help readers reflect about reliable leadership throughout US public education:

- Explain the meaning of "function" as it is conveyed in this chapter.
- How, based on examples taken from this chapter, does function of leadership establish the conditions for reliable public education?
- To what extent are the expectations for education embedded in your daily professional experiences examples of what *ought to be* expectations as they are portrayed in this chapter?
- How does functional educational leadership influence the biomes of a public school?
- Which of the difference-makers identified in this chapter influence reliability to the greatest extent?
- How do you envision reliable leadership and to what extent, if any, does this chapter influence your thinking?

Chapter 12

So Much Leadership, So Little Time

Despite research that indicates the positive impacts of educational leadership, present-day specifications about school leadership cannot be counted upon to enact these impacts effectively for all US students. To make matters worse, educators often turn to management and bureaucracy as if these are the same as leadership (Urick and Bowers, 2014). Hordes of theories, ideologies, and mandates disconnect and distract educational leadership from reliable implementation of the educational environments that all students deserve. Educational leadership is constrained by expectations that distance practice from the original power of education and the values of the moral obligation of public education.

Unreliable educational leadership is a profound dilemma. With so much attention paid to educational leadership and with so little time to accommodate the multitudes of distractions embedded in this frenzied oversight, students in America's public schools are shortchanged if educational leadership does not act on behalf of reliability. Leadership, after all, functions "to confront dilemmas, not let them 'fester and multiply' (Cuban, 1996, 2001; Glatter, 1996)" (Goldring and Greenfield, 2002, p. 12).

At the root of leadership, *leith* means stepping across a threshold and letting go of whatever prevents stepping forward. But, trapped in an indeterminate zone and forestalled by the ideological impositions of free market theory, educators too often stand on the wrong side of the threshold. In the absence of intention, the responsibility of educational leadership to enact the greater good falters.

To step across the threshold and let go of the debilitating, discriminatory, and self-defeating impediments that deny all US students the comprehensive public education they deserve, school leaders have an obligation to reimagine difference-making and intentionality. Letting go of the countless obstacles that prevent fulfillment of the expectation that public education serves all students for the greater good, this concluding chapter presents functional educational leadership as the responsibility that school leaders must, next, undertake. This responsibility is discussed in terms of:

- Responsibility and Obligation: Educational Leadership and the Future.
- Function and Expectations: Educational Leadership and the Future.
- The Ecology of Leadership and the Ecology of Thought.
- Functional Educational Leadership: *The Good* and Democracy.
- Functional Educational Leadership: Working the Work.
- Agentic and Moral Leadership

EDUCATIONAL LEADERSHIP: NOTHING LESS THAN THE FUTURE

Educational leaders sign up for responsibility and obligation. Educational leaders are responsible for nothing less than the future of all students. Educational leaders are obligated to moral agency in the course of fulfilling this responsibility. Public school educators have the capacities and capabilities necessary to fulfill these expectations reliably. But necessary is not the same as sufficient.

It's one thing to have what's necessary for reliable educational leadership. It's another thing to *do* what's both necessary and sufficient to enact reliability as an expectation for leadership. Functional educational leadership enacts the capacities, capabilities, and agency necessary and sufficient for reliability throughout US public education.

Looking for Panaceas in Pandora's Box

Before educational leadership can be reimagined, the misguided and damaging search for educational sure-cures must end.

When present-day practitioners and scholars define educational leadership, their efforts incorporate the worthy ambition to make a difference for US students. Rarely, however, does ambition alone yield difference-making outcomes accurately for all students. Realizing this, educational scholars and practitioners seek, invent, and/or implement theoretical cures for educational unreliability.

Also interested in sure-cures for public education, policymakers, civic leaders, and legislators impose dramatically different perspectives about schooling outcomes of greatest value. These free market-based perspectives—including but not limited to market failure and amorality—are a disservice to students and a roadblock to reliable leadership.

Reliable educational leadership is stymied by nothing less than a search for panaceas in Pandora's Box. Free market cures like standardized tests mold the goals, practices, and expectations espoused by school leaders (Jacobson, 2011). Performance standards are "aimed at driving school improvement forward by changing the practice of school leaders (Barth, 1986; Hallinger and Wimpelberg, 1992)" (Hallinger, 2005, p. 2). Leaping out of Pandora's Box alongside standards and standardized testing are knee-jerk pedagogy, lower-order cognition, and singularity.

Assuming *the* solution lies in panaceas generated by ideology, political imperative, or theory-du-jour leaves devastation in its wake, as Kurth-Schai (2014) indicates:

> increasingly centralized and bureaucratized government mandates (e.g., *No Child Left Behind* and related state legislation); socially acclaimed and aggressively marketed entrepreneurial initiatives (e.g., alternative certification, proprietary charter school chains); powerful special interest lobbies (e.g., test preparation and curriculum development/textbook publishing); and ongoing efforts to further commercialize public spaces (e.g., branded vending and advertising in schools). (p. 424)

Even pursuing a *vision* (a staple of conventional wisdom about effective educational leadership) does nothing more than place "the focus on content rather than process" (Sackney and Mitchell, 2002, p. 900). Present-day investment in panaceas is reflected in research where "most leader behavior studies emphasize how much the behavior is used rather than how well it is used" (Yukl, 2012, p. 75). Dedication to panaceas for educational leadership is a harbinger of unreliability.

EXPECTATIONS, FUNCTION, AND THE FUTURE OF EDUCATIONAL LEADERSHIP

School leaders are uncertain about how best to lead given the forces and factors that derail reliability. In addition, expecting educational leadership to deliver the promises of public education if only the best panacea is identified ignores the ecology of leadership and the ecology of learning environments.

There is no "best" in an ecology. Instead, educational leadership is "best" when what leaders *do* is oriented to nonnegotiable expectations allied with virtue. This orientation is the specification that public educators can rely on to yield accurately the educational environments that engage all students with the original power of education. The agency necessary and sufficient to reliability is function.

When educational leadership is understood as its own ecology, school leaders access the obligation of school leadership: enacting function throughout educational environments to express the original power of education. The ecology of educational environments encompasses several premises:

- *The nonlinear aspect* of teaching and learning. Research demonstrates that increased academic proficiency is "followed by periods of level or slightly declining performance while individuals consolidated their new knowledge and identified the next set of problems on which to focus" (Elmore, 2005, pp. 138–139). Self-correction, reflection, and self-efficacy fuel function of leadership to account for the nonlinear ecology of teaching and learning. Interconnectivities between functions foster reliable student outcomes.
- *The dysfunction of lagging indicators.* Instead of orienting educational environments to the lagging indicators and disconnections within year-to-year fluctuations of test data, self-correction embedded within longitudinal analysis and continuous improvement become barometers calibrated to measure reliable function. Functional educational leadership is process endowed with a "mechanism for self-correction" (English, 2005, p. 84) missing when present-day public education expectations lag behind.
- *Singularity is not ecological.* Reliable educational leadership depends on enacting function from a fundamental understanding that:

    > there is no single or best organization theory. Rather, many possible and enacted theories of organization exist (Gephart, Boje, and Thatchenkery, 1996, p. 2), and theory and practice are as connected to one another as they are to the context and the culture within which they arise. (Sackney and Mitchell, 2002, p. 895)

- *Ecologies are internal/external.* Educational environments reflect, and functional educational leadership recognizes, the imperative for "seeing that problems 'out there' are 'in here' also—and how the two are connected" (Senge, Hamilton, and Kania, 2015, p. 29). Connections are revealed when school leaders learn from the lives of students, their families, their community, and American society. Marginalization, deficit-thinking, and discrimination are both "out there" and "in here"; school leadership is fundamentally unreliable if it is unresponsive to this interface and its detrimental effects.

    Ecologies are *schooling interiorities* which are the "practices and suppositions of work in the school itself" (English, 2005, p. 88). Standards and the learning disconnections inherent in present-day standardized testing focus "solely on the interiorities of schooling for the centering of the standards, [so that] any concept of social justice dealing with the school's exteriorities is vitiated" (English, 2005, p. 87). No school, no leader, can be reliable without confronting this ecological reality.

This view of the ecology of leadership reflects four ecological principles summarized by Wielkiewicz and Stelzner (2005): *interdependence*; *open systems and feedback loops*; *cycling of resources*; and *adaptation* (pp. 326–327).

FUNCTION: THE ECOLOGY OF LEADERSHIP AND THE ECOLOGY OF THOUGHT

An ecology is multitudes of interconnectivities and evolutions to which one style of leadership or some cluster of theories of leadership cannot respond reliably. Expectations necessary for and sufficient to the ecology of leadership underlie the enactment of function. Reimagining educational leadership in this way sustains and improves interconnectivities throughout educational environments to build, improve, and challenge students' ecology of thought:

- Interconnectivities among functions and between school leadership and educational environments immerse educators and students in the original power of education.
- Educators are the *active person* throughout the ecologies of schools as learning environments. The active person expects her/himself to commit to function of leadership as the agency necessary and sufficient for reliability.
- Educators expect self-efficacy from themselves. Self-efficacy derives from the capacities, capabilities, and ecologies of the active person and, for educators, develops from each educator's development of instructional function.
- Educational leadership for the future of teaching and learning that all students deserve has two choices: (1) remain in thrall to the status quo imposed by present-day expectations for school leadership, or, (2) move forward to intend reliability and to function reliably.

Function as Competency

Not only should colleagues, students, parents/caregivers, and citizens expect virtue, moral agency, and function of leadership but school leaders should expect these of themselves. The rationale for this reimagining of educational leadership is provided by Yukl (2002) who notes that "why a leader is effective requires that we examine how different behaviors interact in a mutually consistent way" (Yukl, 2012, p. 76).

Interaction in a mutually consistent way is the competency of function. Reimagining educational leadership as an ecology of interconnectivities puts school leaders in the position of *active person* to enact function. The active person employs *good thinking* which is "the tendency to identify and investigate problems, to probe assumptions, to seek reasons, and to be reflective" (Perkins and Tishman, 2016).

Functions (e.g., dynamic instruction, ethics, emotionally intelligent leadership, and public life education) enacted through good thinking by an active person are integral to educational leadership as an emergent process. Relational, reciprocal, mutual, multidimensional, and continuous, functional educational leadership is an ecology of interconnectivities—beginning with instructional function (see figure 9.1)—capable of evolving educational environments within which teaching and learning evince the original power of education.

When interconnectivities between functions of leadership elicit educational environments in which the original power of education is paramount, reliable leadership develops when:

- *Enacting function* does not depend on one individual to be the only leader in a school or school district. Rather, enacting, as Greenfield (2004) shares in a principal's statement, "*should create conditions that will elicit leadership behaviors from everyone* in the building in circumstances and at times that their contribution is essential for achieving the school's purposes" (emphasis added) (p. 179).

  Elmore (2005) furthers this understanding of the ecology of leadership when he indicates that "individual commitment to collective values requires individuals to choose to have their beliefs, values, and practices influenced by their colleagues and by outside knowledge, and to choose to value collective results over individual results" (p. 136).

  The importance of mutual influence among all school staff as an element in the ecology of leadership echoes the value of "creating a learning organization in which all eyes are focused on leadership for learning" (Seashore Louis, Dretzke, and Wahlstrom, 2010, p. 331). Functional educational leadership can be thought of, thus, as the professional implementation of an ecology in which mutuality, both/and, as well as moral agency thrive.

- *Function is* the activity—fulfillment of the expectations for and moral agency of educational leadership—natural to interconnectivities and professional relationships in reliable public education. Reliability ensues when function of leadership embraces a greater good and establishes the means to enact this objective across multiple ecologies. This is the discernible agency at the core of intentionality.

The ecology of educational leadership is represented, further, in the relationship between functions and a leader's life experience, prior knowledge, context, and instructional function.

FUNCTIONAL EDUCATIONAL LEADERSHIP AND *THE GOOD* AND DEMOCRACY

Public education that immerses all students in the original power of education demands that school leadership is capable of meeting adaptive challenges. Functions of leadership establish this capability; interconnectivities generate virtue-embedded practices and detail-oriented oversight generates message-sensitive reflection.

Functional educational leadership is a process capable of meeting the challenges inherent in *what should be* expected of teaching and learning in public schools. *The good* emerges in exercising the responsibility of public schooling to "develop in young people both the knowledge and skills that individuals need to live free lives and the shared values . . . that citizens need to support the institutions that enable them to live freely" (Gutmann and Ben-Porath, 2015, p. 1).

This understanding incorporates a return to the relationship between public education and democracy as "building a sense of the 'we,' trusting others in shared forms of leadership and knowledge-building, empowering others as publics build capacity to make change, and transcending individualistic frames of knowledge and action (Knight Abowitz, 2014)." (Knight Abowitz, 2018, p. 11). Dynamic instruction, public life education, and ethics interconnect across educational environments in the ecology of thought of all students when enacted by functional educational leadership. The relationship between *the good* and democracy that ought to be alive and well throughout US public education becomes a reliable characteristic of teaching and learning.

The impact of function of leadership lies in the intentionality of a leader's interconnections. Although the term *reliable intentionality* may seem like an oxymoron, the ambition of educators to make a difference in the lives of students reflects this term and is described in the observation that the "final dimension of integrity is conscientiousness, or concern for doing an effective job (Van Der Wal et al., 2011)" (Van Wart, 2013, p. 560).

Conscientiousness or duty associated with functional educational leadership constitutes a "move away from authoritative and individualistic conceptions of the leader by considering leadership as being constituted through the relationships between members of an organization (Crevani et al., 2010)" (Rhodes and Badham, 2018, p. 2). This dimension of integrity fuels function when "leaders understand that duty is important and that it comes with especially high standards in the public sector; duty includes respect for the law, rules, and professional norms (Menzel, 2007; Sergiovanni, 2007; Terry, 1998)" (Van Wart, 2013, p. 560).

Educational Leaders as Moral Agents

The professional norms that undergird functional educational leadership are anchored to conscientiousness, integrity, and virtue. From this foundation, reliability is fostered by school leaders understanding that they function as moral agents. Greenfield (2004) sheds light on the research and scholarship that clarifies how intentionality and function are fostered when leaders are moral agents:

1. Moral agents base their "decisions on principles that apply to classes of situations, not on a whim of the moment or a predilection for one particular kind of situation" (p. 178).
2. Moral agents "consider the welfare and interests of *all* who stand to be affected by [their] decision or action" (p. 178).
3. Moral agents have an obligation to "base [their] decisions on the most complete information relative to the decision that [they] can obtain" (p. 178).
4. Moral agents are conscientious when their examination of a situation yields a prescriptive answer to the question, "What ought I to *do?*" (p. 178).

Agentic Educational Leadership

The issue of reliable school leadership and the role of function of educational leadership in the pursuit of reliability is more than a mere academic enterprise. Practitioners throughout US public education face daunting obstacles to their intentionality. The prevalence of these obstacles and the power of the forces behind these impediments ensures that agentic educational leadership is synonymous with courage. Courage is a matter, among other things, of self-efficacy. Courage is expressed by school leaders as moral agents through the relationship between ethics and competencies.

Function propels self-efficacy; virtue and integrity endow leadership with conscientiousness to enact function courageously. The courage required for function of leadership is found in:

- *Buffering.* A moral agent buffers others from the intrusions that deny students teaching and learning that expresses the original power of education. Kurth-Schai (2014) suggests one instance tailor-made for buffering when

she calls attention to "severe budget cuts that continually threaten children's constitutional rights" (p. 438).
- *Crap-detecting.* Postman and Weingartner (1971) applied this term full force to US public education. This term spotlights the importance of inquiry and authentic learning that engages future citizens—students in US public schools—with the capacities (e.g., principled reasoning, the intelligence of social balance, positive liberty) necessary to detect misdirection, lies, and/or the inverse of social justice. This capacity is a nonnegotiable for citizenship participation in democracy. It is a nonnegotiable fostered by the intentional interconnectivities of functional educational leadership (e.g., ethics, dynamic instruction). School leaders have the obligation to call-out the malfeasance of half-truth and innuendo that public school critics in the age of accountability manufacture about traditional public education (Swensson, Ellis, and Shaffer, 2019a). When students are shortchanged by policy, politics, and ideology, educational leadership is responsible for identifying and combating the imposition of expectations that have nothing to do with the teaching and learning that all students deserve (Hallinger, 2005).
- *De-developing.* In its simplest form, de-development is prioritizing. Leaders in public education who focus on what all students deserve must bring process to bear so that, as Schmoker (2019) indicates, schools "select and focus on only the most urgently needed, evidence-based instructional initiatives" (p. 24). De-development engages school leaders with restoring, through function, the original power of education to US schools while jettisoning present-day mandates and distractions dumped into the laps of overwhelmed, underfunded, and discouraged public schools (Swensson and Shaffer, 2020).
- *Restoring.* Leadership necessary to pursue de-development recognizes not only that public education has been short-circuited by an "addiction to excess" (Schmoker, 2019, p. 26) but that public education has wandered aimlessly for the past several decades without a primary purpose. Restoration of purpose (e.g., engaging all students in the intersection of how to think and the moral obligation of public education) puts public education in position to focus leadership (from all school colleagues) on function to enrich students and their lives once educators have the wherewithal to be intense professionally.
- *Structuring.* Leadership is all about trust. But external accountability (policies, laws, mandates) exhibits little trust in educators. The school leadership that all students deserve cannot fall prey to the imposition of mistrust. Instead, leaders, educators, must practice their profession based on the understanding that, as systems, schools and school districts are self-organizing. This means that educators, leaders, apply educational leadership as

a means of "refocusing the system and allowing it, over time, to organize itself to a better structure given new goals or new constraints" (Rice, 2017, p. 59). Resilience of function of leadership facilitates the reimagining of structure in educational environments.

The Inescapable Dilemma of Leadership

To avoid the misunderstandings and disconnections that afflict present-day thinking about educational leadership and its relationship with US public education, this discussion about functional educational leadership takes account of the inescapable dilemma of leadership.

The inescapable dilemma of leadership is encapsulated in Rhodes and Badham's (2018) observation that the ethical premise of leadership is "an irreconcilable tension between an infinite ethics and a finite practice" (p. 5). Put more prosaically, leadership cannot please all the people all the time. It is inevitable, then, that a functional educational leader "engages in 'grappling with his/her conflicting relationships and responsibilities' such that this 'grappling' is what constitutes the existence of ethical leadership (Rhodes, 2011, p. 1327)" (Rhodes and Badham, 2018, p. 15).

Leaders become responsible for what these scholars refer to as *ethical irony* which denotes "a form of thought, word and deed that recognizes incongruity and contradiction in human affairs, without allowing that incongruity to paralyse action" (Rhodes and Badham, 2018, p. 19). Reliable school leadership that accounts for this conundrum mirrors this five-sentence loop: Leaders reflect. Leaders are ethical. Leaders prioritize. Leaders act. Leaders reflect, this time about acting to restart the loop.

In terms of functional educational leadership, the inescapable dilemma of leadership is encountered ethically by meeting a "'requirement to compare all of the demands [on a leader for ethical behavior], and decide which ones to try to serve, which to neglect or how to compromise between them' (Rhodes, 2012, p. 1324)" (Rhodes and Badham, 2018, p. 15). The interconnectivities among functions (see figure 4.1) provide school leaders with the ethics and competencies necessary and sufficient to endow the finite ways of responding to infinite ethical perspectives and challenges while sustaining educational environments that engage all students with the original power of education.

AGENCY FOR FUNCTIONAL EDUCATIONAL LEADERSHIP

To embrace virtue, confront the inescapable dilemma of leadership, and fuel the original power of education, function becomes instrumental agency, "a tool to do something socially valuable, and predefined in advance" (Matusov, von Duyke, and Kayumova, 2016, p. 426). Functions (comprised of sets as shown in figure 5.2) throughout the double helix (see figure 4.1) express and continuously improve educational leadership. This is agency necessary and sufficient to engage students with *the good* in collective identities, mutuality, I identify as . . . statements, and "we" for successful citizenship participation (see figure 9.1).

Educational leaders enact function (e.g., dynamic instruction, emotionally intelligent leadership) as shown in figure 5.1 to establish the original power of education in the intersection of primary purpose and the values of the moral obligation of public education (Swensson, Ellis, and Shaffer, 2019b; Swensson and Shaffer, 2020).

Educational Expectations Are the Future of Agency

Schools, as Greenfield (2004) reminds us, "are peopled; they are a socially constructed phenomenon that lives in our imaginations, and in our lived experience" (p. 181). The future of agency in educational leadership is the expectation of function. Function suffuses the ecologies of educational environments with social construction of the expectations necessary and sufficient for public life and citizenship participation:

- *The ethic of justice and the ethic of caring:* The dignity of the individual person is the ethic of justice. Attention to the social order and fairness is the ethic of caring. These competencies for virtue ward off singularity and the amorality of the educational marketplace. Reliable educational leadership embraces this expectation as an obligation to a greater good that transcends "individualistic frames of knowledge and action (Knight Abowitz, 2014)" (Knight Abowitz, 2018, p. 11).
- *Complex pedagogies to express the original power of education:* These pedagogies "prepare the environment and facilitate the relationships necessary to support diverse learners as they experience social inquiry, discover shared purpose, and translate collective goals into principled action" (Kurth-Schai, 2014, p. 432). This expectation is derived from instructional function that *ought to be* the foundation for the practice of every public educator. Dynamic instruction incorporates these pedagogies from an understanding that "successful teachers are not simply charismatic, persuasive and expert presenters; rather, they create powerful cognitive and social tasks to their students and teach the students how to make productive use of them" (Hopkins, 2003, p. 61).
- *Interconnectivities and systemic relationships.* Reliable educational leadership depends upon the rungs of the double helix operating "as part of a set

of systemic relationships. Focusing on one without attending to the others is unlikely to bring about sustained improvement" (Hallinger and Heck, 2010, p. 107). Understanding intentionality in this way reveals the applicability of Vygotsky's zone of proximal development to leadership because this notion "refers to functions that have not yet matured but are in the process of maturation" (Sternberg and Grigorenko, 2004, p. 279). Relational agency, interconnectivities and systemic relationships, allow function of leadership to evolve.

FUNCTIONAL EDUCATIONAL LEADERSHIP: WORKING THE WORK

Working the work of reliable educational leadership during the remainder of the twenty-first century demands that school leaders fulfill their obligation to undertake the endlessly difficult task of constructing instructional function. Instructional function serves as a tool of inestimable value within the ecologies of educational environment and educational leadership.

Functional educational leadership, as a result, is within the grasp of every public educator. Instructional function (see figure 5.1) enacts each educator's construction of the intersection between how to think (e.g., independent thinking, positive liberty, principled reasoning) and the moral obligation of public education. Instructional function is the recognition that improved achievement for all students "ultimately depends on improving teaching practice" (Goldring et al., 2007, p. 1).

Instructional function and dynamic instruction represent the work of functional educational leadership necessitated by the unreliability imposed by free market-based standards, testing, mechanisms, and educational practices. School leaders can end the malign influence of these forces and factors by walking beyond the threshold of present-day practices to enact:

- *Intentionality.* Educators' implementation of instructional function demonstrates intentionality, a foundational capacity for functional educational leadership. Intentionality is an educator's thinking disposition which "is a tendency toward a particular pattern of intellectual behavior" (Perkins and Tishman, 2016)
- *Interconnectivity.* Intentionality is comprised of dispositions. *Ability* is identified as "the basic capacity to carry out a behavior [while] inclination concerns the motivation or impulse to engage in the behavior" (Perkins and Tishman, 2016). *Sensitivity* has been described as a bottleneck that delays effective intellectual performance because sensitivity "concerns the likelihood of noticing occasions to engage in" (Perkins and Tishman, 2016) the behavior for which a person already has the ability and inclination.

Instead of a misguided focus on evaluating how many leadership behaviors occur or an equally ineffective assessment of the extent to which school leaders conform to a recipe, the expectation for educational leadership ought to be on *sensitivity*. School leaders have the wherewithal to be sensitive to opportunities and occasions for enacting function to establish reliability.

With their eyes on this prize, America's public educators fulfill the expectation that educational leadership reliably fulfills the role given to *defenders of democracy* (Kurth-Schai, 2014). As such, school leadership "must repeatedly rise to the occasion—adopting a sustained, experimental, and pluralistic approach that supports full and diverse expressions of openness, humility, collaboration, and willingness to grapple with uncertainty and ambiguity (Ansell, 2011; Biesta, 2009; Campbell, 2008; Hytten, 2009)" (Kurth-Schai, 2014, p. 428).

SPEAKING OF FUNCTIONAL EDUCATIONAL LEADERSHIP

Functional educational leadership is a means for constructing educational environments that all students deserve. Several insights speak to functional educational leadership and, in so doing, provide practitioners and researchers with cues and clues to enacting reliable leadership in US public schools.

Although these insights are not the "last word" in this discussion about functional educational leadership, these several notions illuminate the focus of school leaders who turn the tide of unreliability with function:

- Functional educational leadership is "a collaborative relationship instead of a unidirectional influence process from leader to follower" (Wielkiewicz and Stelzner, 2005, p. 330). The interactions and agency of individuals within an ecological system expressed as the intentionality in function of educational leadership describe the process that lies at the core of this reimagining of public school leadership.
- Functional educational leadership empowers public educators with the capacities to meet adaptive challenges. Functions engage all students with principled reasoning, positive liberty, and independent thinking to confront the adaptive challenges that lie ahead.
- Functional educational leadership develops when educators understand "that leadership occurs in a web of interdependent social and biological systems" (Wielkiewicz and Stelzner, 2005, p. 332). The ecology of schools and their biomes are interdependent and complex. Functional school leadership fosters social construction sufficient to the task of systemic reliability of process.

- Functional educational leadership reimagines school leadership as the pattern-seeking device capable of intentional interconnectivities.
- Functional educational leadership develops from "the finding that leadership and capacity building operate as a mutual influence process lends further weight to this perspective on leadership as a highly responsive and contextualised relational process" (Hallinger and Heck, 2010, p. 106).
- Functional educational leadership is a process that "positions leadership at the service of learning" (Sackney and Mitchell, 2002, p. 909).

LOOKING AT THIS BOOK THROUGH THE WINDSHIELD

Functional educational leadership is neither a pure form of school leadership nor, probably, an uncontroversial one. Yet, envisioned as enactment across the rungs of a double helix, functional educational leadership is built on bedrock that supports "schooling [that] will be laden with political values because schooling must always work toward some end . . . [and] . . . any legitimate view of schooling in democratic society will emerge from deliberation among citizens, thoroughly saturated by the values of those citizens" (Murray and Howe, 2017, p. 18).

Functional educational leadership entails commitments, responsibilities, and obligations of educational leadership that are forever a work in progress toward what educational environments *ought to be* on behalf of the futures of all US students. The public work of educators guides the capacities of students to experience citizenship participation in US democracy and, thus, constitutes a greater good facilitated amidst the rungs of functional educational leadership.

From a starting point of virtue, functional educational leadership is "undertaken through open dialogue, accepting interpersonal difference, being accountable to others, public accounting for one's actions, and being reliable (Cunliffe and Ericksen, 2011, p. 1427)" (Rhodes and Badham, 2018, p. 8). Given voice in these ways, functional educational leadership takes a cue from Greenfield (2004) who points out that highly reliable schools "more consistently and reliably accomplish that which we expect of schools" (p. 183).

The expectations that ought to be fundamental to reimagining reliability via functional educational leadership include, but are not limited to:

- Functional educational leadership creates the "most potent sources of power [which] are the shared norms, values, ideals, and beliefs of the participants themselves" (Greenfield, 2004, p. 186).

- Functional educational leadership fosters reliability for "how principals determine when and how to adapt particular leadership practices across multiple contexts" (Klar and Brewer, 2013, p. 34).
- Functional educational leadership emerges, for example, in "the complex connections between a principal's background and past experience, the personal qualities and sensitivities brought to the moment of reflection, and the valuing and intention revealed through action (leading) in a particular school culture and community context" (Greenfield, 2004, p. 189).
- Functional educational leadership is a process that endows agency with resilience. "'A resilient system has a big plateau, a lot of space over which it can wander with gentle elastic walls that will bounce it back, if it comes near a dangerous edge' (Meadows, 2008, p. 78)" (Rice, 2017, p. 59).

Looking at what lies ahead reveals the simple proposition about educational leadership: present-day educational leadership cannot be reliable on behalf of all US public school students because the expectations for teaching and learning are disconnected from the agency and outcomes that all students deserve for school and life success.

All public educators know that all students are capable of learning what is taught. All educators know that when teaching (instructional function) expresses the original power of education to engage students with what is taught, learning outcomes will be reliable. Getting to this point, however, is impeded by a plethora of present-day obstacles.

Educational leadership, as a result, has arrived at a proverbial fork in the road. In one direction, school leaders can continue their professional trek under the baleful influence of factors and forces that prevent educational environments that focus on what all students deserve. In the other direction, educational leadership can let go of present-day strictures to function reliably on behalf of all US students.

Stepping forward to lead, to take teaching and learning well beyond the factors and forces that inflict unreliability on present-day public education, educational leadership must reimagine the issue of how well leadership is used or applied. This issue, the centerpiece of reliability, is largely uncharted territory.

Choosing to confront uncharted territory will always be part of school leadership. Uncharted territory is not only the bread-and-butter of school leadership but it is also an ecology of the future tailor-made for functional educational leadership. If school leaders continue to choose to acquiesce to the daunting and disastrous factors that assail present-day public education, few will notice. But if educational leadership is reimagined by practitioners and scholars as *doing* functional educational leadership, reliable teaching and learning alongside robust futures for all public school students can develop.

Educational leadership in America's public schools is at a crossroad. School leaders are capable and the reimagining of leadership necessary and sufficient to serve all students is well within their capacities. Whether functional educational leadership is enacted and whether reliability is returned to the educational environments of US public schools is now a matter for leading, crossing the threshold of disconnected practice and discarding the factors that deny all students the learning they deserve.

References

Abrahams, D. S. (2007). Emotional Intelligence and Army Leadership: Give It to Me Straight! *Military Review*, March–April, 2007. Retrieved from www.armyupress.army.mil.

Amanchukwu, R. N., Stanley, G. J., and Ololube, N. P. (2015). A Review of Leadership Theories, Principles and Styles and their Relevance to Educational Management. *Management* 5(1), 6–14. doi:10.5923/j.mm.20150501.02.

Ancona, D., Malone, T. W., Orlikowski, W. J., and Senge, P. M. (2011). In Praise of the Incomplete Leader. In *HBR's 10 Must Reads: On Leadership*, 176–196. Boston, MA: Harvard Business Review Press.

Balyer, A. (2017). Trust in School Principals: Teachers' Opinions. *Journal of Education and Learning* 6(2), 317–325. doi:10:5539/jel.v6n2p317.

Bandura, A. (1983). Self-Efficacy Determinants of Anticipated Fears and Calamities. *Journal of Personality and Social Psychology* 45(2), 464–469.

Beare, H., Caldwell, B. J., and Millikan, R. H. (1989). *Creating an Excellent School: Some New Management Techniques*. London: Routledge.

Beatty, B. R. (2000). Emotional Matters in Educational Leadership. Paper presented to the *Australian Association for Research in Education Annual Conference*, Sydney, Australia, December 3–8, 2000. Toronto, Ontario, Canada: Ontario Institute for Studies in Education.

Bossert, S. T., Dwyer, B. C., Rowan, B., and Lee, G. (1982). The Instructional Management Role of the Principal. *Educational Administration Quarterly* 18, 34–64.

Bottery, M. (1992). *The Ethics of Educational Management: Personal, Social and Political Perspectives on School Organization*. London, UK: Cassell Educational.

Boyte, H. C. (2011). Constructive Politics as Public Work: Organizing the Literature. *Political Theory* 39(5), 630–660. doi:10.1177/0090591711413747.

Boyte, H. C. (2013). Reinventing Citizenship as Public Work. *Civic Engagement*, Paper 31. Retrieved from http://digitalcommons.unomaha.edu/slceciviceng31.

Bronfenbrenner, U. (1979). *The Ecology of Human Development: Experiments by Nature and Design*. Cambridge, MA: Harvard University Press.

Brooks, J. S., Knaus, C. B., and Chang, H. (2015). Educational Leadership Against Racism: Challenging Policy, Pedagogy, and Practice. *International Journal of Multicultural Education* 17(1), 1–5.

Brown v. Board of Education, 347 U.S. 483 (1954).

Buchanan, J. M. (1979). Natural and artefactual man. In James M. Buchanan (Ed.), *What Should Economists Do?*, 93–112. Indianapolis, IN: Liberty Press.

Campbell, E. (2008). Teaching Ethically as a Moral Condition of Professionalism. In Larry P. Nucci and Darcia Narvaez (Eds.), *Handbook of Moral and Character Education*, 601–615. New York, NY: Routledge.

Capper, C. A., and Green, T. L. (2013). Organizational Theories and the Development of Leadership Capacity for Integrated, Socially Just Schools. In Linda C. Tillman and James Joseph Scheurich (Eds.), *Handbook of Research on Educational Leadership for Equity and Diversity*, 62–82. New York, NY: Routledge.

Chambers, T. V., Huggins, K. S., Locke, L. A., and Fowler, R. M. (2014). Between a "ROC" and a School Place: The Role of *Racial Opportunity Cost* in the Educational Experiences of Academically Successful Students of Color. *Educational Studies* 50, 464–497. doi:10.1080/00131946.2014.943891.

Ciulla, J. B., Knights, D., Mabey, C., and Tomkins, L. (2018). Philosophical Contributions to Leadership Ethics. *Business Ethics Quarterly* 28(1), 1–14. doi:10.1017/beq.2017.48.

Cohen, J., McCabe, E. M., Michelli, N. M., and Pickeral, T. (2009). School Climate: Research, Policy, Practice, and Teacher Education. *Teachers College Record* 111(1), 180–213.

Cohen-Vogel, L., and Harrison, C. (2013). Leading with Data: Evidence from the National Center on Scaling up Effective Schools. *Leadership and Policy in Schools* 12, 122–145. doi:10.1080/15700763.2013.792934.

Cordeiro, P. A., and Cunningham, W. G. (2013). *Educational Leadership: A Bridge to Improved Practice*, 5th Edition. Boston, MA: Pearson.

Daly, A. J. (2009). Rigid Response in an Age of Accountability: The Potential of Leadership and Trust. *Educational Administration Quarterly* 45(2), 168–216. doi:10.1177/0013161X08330499.

Darling, N. (2007). Ecological Systems Theory: The Person in the Center of the Circles. *Research in Human Development* 4(3–4), 203–217.

DeMatthews, D. E. (2014). How to Improve Curriculum Leadership: Integrating Leadership Theory and Management Strategies. *The Clearing House* 87, 192–196. doi:10.1080/00098655.2014.911141.

Deming, W. E. (1989). *Out of the Crisis. Quality, Productivity and Competitive Position*. Cambridge, MA: MIT Press.

Dewey, J. (1916). *Democracy and Education*. Retrieved from www.public-library.uk.

Dewey, J. (1933). *How We Think*. Boston, MA: D. C. Heath.

Dewey, J. (1937). Education and Social Change. *Social Frontier* 3, 235–238.

Douglass, A. (2018). Redefining Leadership: Lessons from an Early Education Leadership Development Initiative. *Early Childhood Education Journal* 46, 387–396. doi:10.1007/s10643-017-0871-9.

Eagly, A. H., and Chin, J. L. (2010). Diversity and Leadership in a Changing World. *American Psychologist* 65(3), 216–224. doi:10.1037/z0018957.

Elmore, R. F. (2005). Accountable Leadership. *The Educational Forum* 69, 134–142.

English, F. W. (2005). Educational Leadership for Sale: Social Justice, the ISLLC Standards, and the Corporate Assault on Public Schools. In T. Creighton, S. Harris, and J. Coleman (Eds.), *Crediting the Past, Challenging the Present, Creating the Future*, 81–104. Houston, TX: National Council of Professors of Educational Administration.

English, F. W. (Ed.). (2006). *Encyclopedia of Educational Leadership and Administration*, Vol. 1. Thousand Oaks, CA: Sage Publications.

English, F. W. (Ed.). (2006). *Encyclopedia of Educational Leadership and Administration*, Vol. 2. Thousand Oaks, CA: Sage Publications.

Fernandez, S. (2005). Developing and Testing an Integrative Framework of Public Sector Leadership: Evidence from the Public Education Arena. *Journal of Public Administration Research and Theory* 15(2), 197–217.

Fisher, D., and Frey, N. (2008). *Better Learning through Structured Teaching: A Framework for the Gradual Release of Responsibility*. Alexandria, VA: ASCD.

Forner, M., Bierlein-Palmer, L., and Reeves, P. (2012). Leadership Practices of Effective Rural Superintendents: Connections to Waters and Marzano's Leadership Correlates. *Journal of Research in Rural Education* 27(8), 1–13. Retrieved from http://jrre./psu/edu/articles/27-8.

Fraise, N. J., and Brooks, J. S. (2015). Toward a Theory of Culturally Relevant Leadership for School-Community Culture. *International Journal of Multicultural Education* 17(1), 6–21.

Fraser-Burgess, S. (2012). Group Identity, Deliberative Democracy, and Diversity in Education. *Educational Philosophy and Theory* 44(5), 480–501. doi:10.1111/j.1469-5812.2010.00717.x.

Gardner, H. (1983). *Frames of Mind: The Theory of Multiple Intelligences*. New York, NY: Basic Books.

General Motors. (1957). *Adventures of the Inquiring Mind*. Detroit, MI: Public Relations Department of General Motors.

Goldring, E., and Greenfield, W. (2002). Understanding the Evolving Concept of Leadership in Education: Roles, Expectations, and Dilemmas. In J. Murphy (Ed.), *The Educational Leadership Challenge: Redefining Leadership for the 21st Century*, 1–19. Chicago, IL: University of Chicago Press.

Goldring, E., Porter, A., Murphy, J., Elliott, S. N., and Cravens, X. (2007). Assessing Learning-Centered Leadership: Connections to Research, Professional Standards, and Current Practices. Prepared for the *Wallace Foundation Grant on Leadership Assessment*, March 1–27, 2007.

Goldstein, D. (2015). *The Teacher Wars: A History of America's Most Embattled Profession*. New York, NY: Anchor Books.

Goleman, D. (2000). Leadership that Gets Results. In *HBR's Must-Reads on Managing People*, 2–17. Cambridge, MA: Harvard Business School Publishing Corporation.

Goleman, D., Boyatzis, R., and McKee, A. (2004). *Primal Leadership: Learning to Lead with Emotional Intelligence*. Cambridge, MA: Harvard Business School Press.

Goleman, D. (2011). What Makes a Leader? In *HBR's 10 Must Reads: On Leadership*, 1–21. Boston, MA: Harvard Business Review Press.

Gray, D. (2009). Emotional Intelligence and School Leadership. *The Connexions Project*. Retrieved from http://cnx.org/m32314/1.1.

Greenfield, Jr., W. D. (2004). Moral Leadership in Schools. *Journal of Educational Administration* 42(2), 174–196. doi:10.1108095782304105525595.

Gutmann, A., and Ben-Porah, S. (2015). Democratic Education. In Michael T. Gibbons (Ed.), *The Encyclopedia of Political Thought*, 1–12. West Sussex, UK: John Wiley & Sons, Ltd.

Hallinger, P. (2005). Instructional Leadership and the School Principal: A Passing Fancy that Refuses to Fade Away. *Leadership and Policy in Schools* 4(1), 1–20. doi:10.1080/15700760500244793.

Hallinger, P., and Heck, R. H. (2002). What Do You Call People with Visions? The Role of Vision, Mission and Goals in School Leadership and Improvement. In Kenneth Leithwood and Philip Hallinger (Eds.), *Second International Handbook of Educational Leadership and Administration, Part One*, 9–40. Dordrecht, The Netherlands: Kluwer Academic Publishers.

Hallinger, P., and Heck, R. H. (2010). Collaborative Leadership and School Improvement: Understanding the Impact on School Capacity and Student Learning. *School Leadership and Management* 30(2), 95–110. doi:10.1080/31003663214136324.

Harris, A., Day, C., Hadfield, M., Hopkins, D., Hargreaves, A., and Chapman, C. (2003). *Effective Leadership for School Improvement*. London: RoutledgeFalmer.

Hersey, H., and Blanchard, K. H. (1977). *Management of Organizational Behavior: Utilizing Human Resources*, 3rd Edition. Englewood Cliffs, NJ: Prentice Hall.

Hoffman, J. D., Ivcevic, Z., and Brackett, M. A. (2018). Building Emotionally Intelligent Schools: From Preschool to High School and Beyond. In Kateryna V. Keefer, James D. A. Parker, and Donald H. Saklofske (Eds.), *Emotional Intelligence in Education: Integrating Research with Practice*, 173–198. Cham, Switzerland: Springer.

Hopkins, D. (2003). Instructional Leadership and School Improvement. In Alma Harris et al. (Eds.), *Effective Leadership for School Improvement*, 112–135. London: RoutledgeFalmer.

Ingersoll, R. M., and Collins, G. J. (2017). *Journal of Curriculum Studies* 49(1), 75–95. doi:10.1080/00220272.2016.1205142.

Jacobson, S. (2011). Leadership Effects on Student Achievement and Sustained School Success. *International Journal of Educational Management* 25(1), 33–44. doi:10.1108/09513541111100107.

Johnson, Jr., J. F., and Willis, C. (2013). Culturally Responsive Teaching and High-Performing Schools that Serve Diverse Populations. In Linda C. Tillman and James Joseph Scheurich (Eds.), *Handbook of Research on Educational Leadership for Equity and Diversity*, 436–458. New York, NY: Routledge.

Kersten, T., Trybus, M., and White, D. (2009). Improving Administrative Internship Programs: Perceptions of Illinois Principals. *Connexions*. Retrieved from http://cnx.org/content/m23291/1.1/.

Klar, H. W., and Brewer, C. A. (2013). Successful Leadership in High Needs Schools: An Examination of Core Leadership Practices Enacted in Challenging Contexts. *Educational Administration Quarterly* 49(5), 1–41. doi:10.1177/0013161X13482577.

Knight Abowitz, K. (2018). The War on Public Education: Agonist Democracy and the Fight for Schools as Public Things. *Philosophical Inquiry in Education* 25(1), 1–15.

Knight Abowitz, K., and Stitzlein, S. M. (2018). Public Schools, Public Goods, and Public Work. *Kappan* 100(3), 33–37.

Kotter, J. P. (2011). What Leaders Really Do. In *HBR's 10 Must Reads: On Leadership*, 37–56. Boston, MA: Harvard Business Review Press.

Kurth-Schai, R. (2014). Fidelity in Public Education Policy: Reclaiming the Deweyan Dream. *Educational Studies* 50, 420–446. doi:10.1080/00131946.2014.943892.

Labaree, D. F. (2018). Public Schools for Private Gain: The Declining American Commitment to Serving the Public Good. *Kappan* 100(3), 8–13.

Labby, S., Lunenburg, F. C., and Slate, J. R. (2012). Emotional Intelligence and Academic Success: A Conceptual Analysis for Educational Leaders. *International Journal of Educational Leadership Preparation* 7(1), 1–12.

Ladson-Billings, G. (2006). From the Achievement Gap to the Education Debt: Understanding Achievement in U.S. Schools. *Educational Researcher* 35(7), 3–12.

Lapsley, D. K. (2008). Moral Self-Identity and the Aim of Education. In Larry P. Nucci and Darcia Narvaez (Eds.), *Handbook of Moral and Character Education*, 30–50. New York, NY: Routledge.

Larsson, J., and Vinberg, S. (2010). Leadership Behavior in Successful Organisations: Universal or Situation-Dependent? *Total Quality Management* 21(3), 317–334. doi:10.1080/14783360903561779.

Latta, G. F. (2019). Cracking the Code of Distributed Leadership: New Insights from a Study of Leader Practitioners. *Journal of Management Policy and Practice* 20(2), 75–92.

Lehman, L. (2013). Principal Internships in Indiana: A Promising or Perilous Experience? *International Journal of Educational Leadership Preparation* 8(1), 121–139.

Leithwood, K. (1999). An Organizational Perspective on Values for Leaders of Future Schools. In Paul Thomas Begley (Ed.), *Values and Educational Leadership*, 25–50. Albany, NY: SUNY Press.

Leithwood, K., Harris, A., and Hopkins, D. (2008). Seven Strong Claims about Successful School Leadership. *School Leadership and Management* 28(1), 27–42. doi:10.1080/13632430701800060.

Lowery, L. F. (1998). *The Biological Basis of Thinking and Learning, Monograph*, 1–22. Full Option Science System. Berkeley, CA: The Regents of the University of California.

Lubienski, C. (2013). Privatizing Form or Function? Equity, Outcomes and Influence in America's Charter Schools. *Oxford Review of Education* 39(4), 498–513. doi:10.1080/03054985.2013.821853.

Marzano, R. J., Waters, T., and McNulty, B. (2005). *School Leadership that Works: From Research to Results*. Alexandria, VA: Association for Supervision and Curriculum Development.

Matusov, E., von Duyke, K., and Kayumova, S. (2016). Mapping Concepts of Agency in Educational Contexts. *Integrative Psychology and Behavioral Science* 50, 420–446. doi:10.1007/s12124-015-9336-0.

Mayer, J. (2017). *Dark Money: The Hidden History of the Billionaires Behind the Rise of the Radical Right*. New York, NY: Anchor Books.

McWilliam, E. (2008). Unlearning How to Teach. *Innovations in Education and Teaching International* 45(3), 263–269. doi:10.1080/14703290802176147.

Minkos, M. L., Sassu, K. A., Gregory, J. L., Patwa, S. S., Theodore, L. A., and Femc-Bagwell, M. (2017). Culturally Responsive Practice and the Role of School Administrators. *Psychology in the Schools* 54, 1260–1266. doi:10.1002/pits.22072.

Mitchell, R. M., Kensler, L., and Tschannen-Moran, M. (2016, in Press). Student Trust in Teachers and Student Perceptions of Safety: Positive Predictors of Student Identification with School. *International Journal of Leadership in Education*.

Moore, B. (2009). Emotional Intelligence for School Administrators: A Priority for School Reform? *American Secondary Education* 37(3), 20–27.

Murphy, J. (2003). Reculturing Educational Leadership: The ISLLC Standards Ten Years Out. *Paper Prepared for the National Policy Board for Educational Administration*. Fairfax, VA: National Policy Board for Educational Administration.

Murphy, J., Neumerski, C. M., Goldring, E., Grissom, J., and Porter, A. (2016). Bottling Fog? The Quest for Instructional Management. *Cambridge Journal of Education* 46(4), 455–471. doi:10.1080/0305764X.2015.1064096.

Murphy, J., Seashore Louis, K., and Smylie, M. (2017). Positive School leadership: How the Professional Standards for Educational Leaders Can Be Brought to Life. *Kappan* 99(1), 21–24.

Murray, K., and Howe, K. R. (2017). Neglecting Democracy in Education Policy: A-F School Report Card Accountability Systems. *Education Policy Analysis Archives* 25(109), 2–22. doi:10.14507/epaa.25.3017.

NPBEA (National Policy Board for Educational Administration. (nd). *PSEL (Professional Standards for Educational Leaders)*. Retrieved from www.npbea.org.

NPBEA (National Policy Board for Educational Administration). (2015). *Professional Standards for Educational Leaders*. Reston, VA: Author.

Nathanson, L., Rivers, S. E., Flynn, L. M., and Brackett, M. A. (2016). Creating Emotionally Intelligent Schools with RULER. *Emotion Review* 8(4), 1–6. doi:10.1177/1754073916650495.

National Commission on Excellence in Education. (1983). *A Nation at Risk: The Imperative for Educational Reform*. Washington, DC: United States Department of Education.

Northouse, P. G. (2007). Culture and Leadership. In Peter G. Northouse (Ed.), *Leadership: Theory and Practice*, 335–376. Thousand Oaks, CA: Sage Publications.

Nucci, L. P. (2008). Social Cognitive Domain Theory and Moral Education. In Larry P. Nucci and Darcia Narvaez (Eds.), *Handbook of Moral and Character Education*, 291–309. New York, NY: Routledge.

Nutt, P. C. (2004). Organizational De-development. *Journal of Management Studies* 41(7), 1083–1103.

Ogbu, J. U. (2004). Collective Identity and the Burden of "Acting White" in Black History, Community, and Education. *The Urban Review* 36(1), 1–35.

Orazi, D. C., Turrini, A., and Valotti, G. (2013). Public Sector Leadership: New Perspectives for Research and Practice. *International Review of Administrative Sciences* 79(3), 486–504. doi:10.1177/0020852313489945.

Owens, R. G., and Valesky, T. C. (2011). *Organizational Behavior in Education: Leadership and School Reform*, 10th Edition. Boston, MA: Pearson.

Park, S., Hironaka, S., Carver, P., and Nordstrum, L. (2013). *Continuous Improvement in Education. White Paper*. New York, NY: Carnegie Foundation for the Advancement of Teaching.

Perkins, D., and Tishman, S. (2001). Dispositional Aspects of Intelligence. In Janet M. Collis and Samuel Messick (Eds.), *Intelligence and Personality: Bridging the Gap in Theory and Measurement*, 233–257. Mahwah, NJ: Lawrence Erlbaum Associates.

Perkins, D., and Tishman, S. (2016). Patterns of Thinking: An Investigation into the Nature of Critical and Creative Thinking. *Project Zero Overview*. Cambridge, MA: Harvard Graduate School of Education.

Postman, N., and Weingartner, C. (1971). *Teaching as a Subversive Activity*. New York, NY: Delta.

Powers, Richard. (2018). *The Overstory*. New York, NY: W. W. Norton & Company.

Putnam, R. D. (1993). The Prosperous Community: Social Capital and Public Life. *The American Prospect* 4(13), 1–11.

Quin, J., Deris, A., Bischoff, G., and Johnson, J. T. (2015). Comparison of Transformational Leadership Practices: Implications for School Districts and Principal Preparation Programs. *Journal of Leadership Education* 49(2), 125–142. doi:1012806/V14/I3/R5.

Ravitch, D. (2020). *Slaying Goliath: The Passionate Resistance to Privatization and the Fight to Save America's Public Schools*. New York, NY: Alfred A. Knopf.

Reimers, F. (2006). Citizenship, Identity and Education: Examining the Public Purposes of Schools in an Age of Globalization. *Prospects* 36(3), 275–294.

Reisch, M. (2002). Defining Social Justice in a Socially Unjust World. *Families in Society: The Journal of Contemporary Human Services* 83(4), 343–354.

Rhodes, C., and Badham, R. (2018). Ethical Irony and the Relational Leader: Grappling with the Infinity of Ethics and Finitude of Practice. *Business Ethics Quarterly* 28(1), 71–98.

Rosenthal, S. A., and Pittinsky, T. L. (2006). Narcissistic Leadership. *The Leadership Quarterly* 17, 617–633.

Rice, J. (2017). The Disconnect Between Heralded Business Concepts and Effective School Leadership. *Educational Planning* 24(2), 55–61.

Riggio, R. E., and Reichard, R. J. (2008). The Emotional and Social Intelligences of Effective Leadership. *Journal of Managerial Psychology* 23(2), 169–185. doi:10.1108/02683940810850808.

Sackney, L., and Mitchell, C. (2002). Postmodern Expressions of Educational Leadership. In Kenneth Leithwood and Philip Hallinger (Eds.), *Second International Handbook of Educational Leadership and Administration, Part Two*, 881–913. Dordrecht, The Netherlands: Kluwer Academic Publishers.

Santamaria, L. J. (2013). Critical Change for the Greater Good: Multicultural Perceptions in Educational Leadership Toward Social Justice and Equity. *Educational Administration Quarterly* 50(3), 347–391.

Santamaria, L. J., and Santamaria, A. P. (2015). Counteracting Educational Injustice with Applied Critical Leadership: Culturally Responsive Practices Promoting Sustainable Change. *International Journal of Multicultural Education* 17(1), 22–42.

Schmoker, M. (2019). Embracing the Power of Less. *Educational Leadership* 76(6), 24–29.

Scott, D. (2018). Why Does School Leadership Matter? *Special Report. School Leadership: A Primer for Policymakers*. Denver, CO: Education Commission of the States. Retrieved from www.esc.org.

Seashore Louis, K., Dretzke, B., and Wahlstrom, K. (2010). How Does Leadership Affect Student Achievement? Results from a National US Survey. *School Effectiveness and School Improvement* 21(3), 315–336. doi:10.1080/09243453.2010.486586.

Senge, P. (1990). *The Fifth Discipline: The Art and Practice of the Learning Organization*. New York, NY: Currency Doubleday.

Senge, P., Hamilton, H., and Kania, J. (2015). The Dawn of System Leadership. *Stanford Social Innovation Review* 13, 27–33.

Shaffer, M. B., and Dincher, B. (2020). In Indiana, School Choice Means Segregation. *Kappan* 101(5), 40–43. doi:10.1177/0031721720903827.

Sommers, M. K. (2016). The Power of Emotional Intelligence. *NAESP Communicator* 39(11), 32.

Spillane, J. P., Parise, L. M., and Zoltners Sherer, J. (2011). Organizational Routines as Coupling Mechanisms: Policy, School Administration, and the Technical Core. *American Educational Research Journal* 48(3), 586–619. doi:10.3102/0002831210385102.

Spreier, S. W., Fontaine, M. H., and Malloy, R. L. (2006, June). Leadership Run Amok: The Destructive Potential of Overachievers. *Harvard Business Review* 84, 72–82.

Stefkovich, J., and Begley, P. T. (2007). Ethical School Leadership: Defining the Best Interests of Students. *Educational Management Administration & Leadership* 35(2), 205–224. doi:10.1177/1741143207075389.

Sternberg, R. J. (2017, January). Testing for Better and Worse. *Phi Delta Kappan* 98(4), 66–71.

Sternberg, R. J., and Grigorenko, E. L. (2004). Successful Intelligence in the Classroom. *Theory into Practice* 43(4), 274–280. Retrieved from www.tandfonline.com/doi/abs/10.1207/s15430421tip4304_5.

Suitts, S. (2019, June 4). Segregationists, Libertarians, and the Modern "School Choice" Movement. Monograph. *Southern Spaces*. Retrieved from www.southernspaces.org.

Sun, R., and Henderson, A. C. (2017). Transformational Leadership and Organizational Processes: Influencing Public Performance. *Public Administration Review* 77(4), 554–565. doi:10.1111/puar.12654.

Swensson, J., Ellis, J., and Shaffer, M. (2019a). *Unraveling Reform Rhetoric: What Educators Need to Know and Understand*. London: Rowman & Littlefield.

Swensson, J., Ellis, J., and Shaffer, M. (2019b). *An Educator's GPS: Fending Off the Free Market of Schooling for America's Students*. London: Rowman & Littlefield.

Swensson, J., and Shaffer, M. (2020). *Defining the Good School: Educational Adequacy Is More Than Minimums*. London: Rowman & Littlefield.

Tench, R. (2016). Emotional Intelligence: An Essential Leadership Trait for Educators. *The William & Mary Educational Review* 4(1), 4–6.

Theoharis, G. (2009). *The School Leaders Our Children Deserve: Seven Keys to Equity, Social Justice, and School Reform*. New York, NY: Teachers College Press.

Urick, A. (2016). Examining US Principal Perception of Multiple Leadership Styles Used to Practice Shared Instructional Leadership. *Journal of Educational Administration* 54(2), 152–172. doi:10.1108/JEA-07-2014-0088.

Urick, A., and Bowers, A. J. (2014). What Are the Different Types of Principals Across the United States? A Latent Class Analysis of Principal Perception of Leadership. *Educational Administration Quarterly* 50(1), 96–134. doi:10.1177/0013161X13489019.

Van Rooy, D. L., and Viswesvaran, C. (2004). Emotional Intelligence: A Meta-Analytic Investigation of Predictive Validity and Nomological Net. *Journal of Vocational Behavior* 65, 71–95. doi:10.1016/S0001-8791(03)00076-9.

Van Wart, M. (2013). Lessons from Leadership Theory and the Contemporary Challenges of Leaders. *Public Administration Review* 73(4), 553–565. doi:10.1111/puar.12069.

Wahlstrom, K. L., and Seashore Louis, K. (2008). How Teachers Experience Principal Leadership: The Roles of Professional Community, Trust, Efficacy, and Shared Responsibility. *Educational Administration Quarterly* 44(4), 458–495. doi:10.1177/0013161X08321502.

Waldman, A. (2019). How Teach for America Evolved into an Arm of the Charter School Movement. *ProPublica*. Retrieved from www.propublica.org.

Waters, J. T., and Marzano, R. J. (2007, Spring). School District Leadership That Works: The Effect of Superintendent Leadership on Achievement. *ERS Spectrum* 25(2), 1–12.

Wielkiewicz, R. M., and Stelzner, S. P. (2005). An Ecological Perspective on Leadership Theory, Research, and Practice. *Review of General Psychology* 9(4), 326–341. doi:10.1037/1089-2680.9.4.326.

Yukl, G. (2012). Effective Leadership Behavior: What We Know and What Questions Need More Attention. *Academy of Management Perspectives* 26(4), 66–85. doi:10.5465/amp.2012.0088.

Zeidner, M., Matthews, B., and Roberts, R. D. (2009). Schooling Emotional Intelligence. In Moshe Zeidner, Bernard Matthews, and Richard D. Roberts (Eds.), *What We Know About Emotional Intelligence: How It Affects Learning, Relationships, and Our Mental Health*, 225–252. Cambridge, MA: The MIT Press.

Zins, J. E., Bloodworth, M. R., Weissberg, R. P., and Walberg, H. J. (2004). The Scientific Base Linking Social and Emotional Learning to School Success. In Joseph E. Zins, Michelle R. Bloodworth, Roger P. Weissberg, and Herbert J. Walberg (Eds.), *Building Academic Success on Social and Emotional Learning: What Does Research Say?*, 1–22. New York, NY: Teachers College Press.

Zucker, R. (2019). Why Highly Efficient Leaders Fail. *HBR Podcasts*, February 12, 2019.

Index

ability, 12
accountability, 18, 38, 59, 108, 110; external, 115; internal, 77
active learning, 56, 57; loop of, 57
active person, 132, 133, 143
adaptive challenges, 40, 130
agency, 6, 44, 61, 66, 90, 102, 146, 153
American Legislative Exchange Council (ALEC), 19

Brown v. Board, 71
Business Roundtable, 19

change, 11, 36, 116, 135
charismatic leadership, 16, 36
charter schools, 18, 109
citizenship, 94, 100; education for, 93, 95; participation in, 111, 129, 147
classical bureaucratic theory, 4, 20, 31
collective identity, 95, 100
competency, 7, 8

DCaR. *See* dissent, conflict, and resolution
de-development, 11, 147
default culture of public education, 60
deficit thinking, 72, 131
democracy, 8, 70, 93, 102, 123, 145, 151
details, 117; anticipation of, 118; evaluation of, 119
dissent, 102, 104; dissent, conflict, and resolution (DCaR), 103
double helix, 45, 46, 67, 152; rungs of, 47, 76, 79
dynamic instruction, 53, 55, 57, 62, 66, 88, 102, 149

echo leadership, 110
ecological systems theory, 25, 44, 46, 130, 143
educational environment, 56, 71, 79, 115, 128, 142, 147; ecology of, 111, 112, 141
educational leadership, 5, 7, 9, 20, 23, 31, 38, 73, 78, 90, 108, 115, 128, 147; agency of, 6; commitments, 21, 116; dedication to, 6; definition of, 5; ecology of, 38, 44, 130, 133, 142, 144, 153; ethics of, 6, 7, 72; evaluation of, 31, 135; expectations of, 54, 78, 129, 131, 136, 139; history of, 5, 17; moral agency of, 21; obligations of, 6, 21, 22, 79, 140, 147; process of, 131, 132; purpose of, 25; relationships with, 5, 8, 9, 74, 83, 128; reliability of, 24, 131, 136, 144; responsibilities of, 8, 16, 23, 57,

66, 75, 76, 100; styles of, 12, 30, 35; theoretical overlap of, 37; theories of, 9, 20, 29, 31, 33, 34, 49; worth of, 7
efficiency, 17, 109
emergent process, 39, 144
emotional intelligence, 80, 83, 84, 87, 89; abilities of, 85, 86, 91; definition of, 82; limbic system and, 87, 91
ethics, 21, 69, 76, 79, 119, 129, 148, 149; *being* ethical, 70, 73, 75, 78; history of, 71; irony of, 148
eye on the prize, 56, 133

freedom vis-à-vis learning, 79, 101
free market: schooling, 10, 73, 99, 141; theory, 18, 60, 72, 108, 109, 139
function, 12, 43, 44, 47, 50, 60, 75, 91, 101, 109, 113, 114, 124, 134, 136, 144; expectations of, 135
functional educational leadership, 26, 39, 47, 61, 86, 90, 100, 107, 111, 112, 124, 132, 136, 140, 148, 149, 151

ghost leadership, 10
the good, 5, 8, 23, 101, 132, 145, 149

habits of public creation, 96, 102, 104
highly reliable educational leadership (HREL), 128, 133, 134
how to think, 56
HREL. *See* highly reliable educational leadership
human capital, 90

indeterminate zone, 39, 44, 108, 132
instructional function, 132, 133, 144, 150
instructional leadership, 54, 59
integrity, 75, 77, 145
intelligence, 82, 85; of common good, 101, 104; of social balance, 97, 130
intentionality, 77, 85, 90, 111, 150

interconnectivity, 65, 113, 136, 143, 149, 150
islanding, 98, 99

leadership, 4, 8; definition of, 4; differential in, 65; history of, 4, 5; inescapable dilemma of, 148; styles of, 11, 29
leadership *for instruction*, 53, 56, 62
leadership *of instruction*, 53, 55, 63
lead-out, 22, 57, 135
learning, 57

management, 4, 24, 33, 36, 82, 139
marginalization, 72
morality, 21, 78, 123, 146
mutuality, 95, 103, 129

narcissistic leadership, 15
A Nation at Risk, 18
No Child Left Behind (NCLB), 108
norms, 13, 17, 23, 146

old growth educational leadership theories, 29, 31
organizational leadership, 17, 82
original power of education, 57, 58, 65, 113, 131, 149
over-choice, 9

pattern-seeking device, 12
pedagogies, 67; complex, 63, 149; soundly structured, 63
positional leadership, 15
presence, 104
principal, 10, 16, 53, 54, 124
privatization, 18
process, 151, 152
pseudotransformational leadership, 19
public education, 95
public good, 18, 31, 97
public life, 95, 96, 98, 149; education, 100, 101, 102

public things, 43, 101, 104
public work, 113, 152

racial opportunity cost, 72
reflection, 76, 77, 142
reform, 11, 66, 110, 115
reliability, 9, 13, 26, 127, 152
reliable educational leadership, 5, 48

scientific management, 4, 31
second growth educational leadership theories, 29, 33
SEL. *See* social and emotional learning
self-efficacy, 64, 75, 91, 142
sensitivity, 12, 91, 151
singularity, 73, 90, 98, 129, 135, 142
social and emotional learning (SEL), 88

social construction, 15, 26, 102, 151
social contract, 77
social justice, 72
standardized testing, 19, 59
standards, 18, 19, 109, 141
students, 13, 19, 60, 64, 72, 78, 88, 123, 135, 145
subjective constructs, 21

test prep, 59
trust, 103, 119

universal audience, 19

virtue, 6, 8, 16, 22, 74, 129; definition of, 7

Who's the Greatest One of All (WGOA) Syndrome, 20, 73

About the Authors

Jeff Swensson, PhD, retired from Ball State University after serving as assistant professor in the Department of Educational Leadership. His career before teaching at Ball State included:

- Superintendent, Carmel Clay (IN) Schools
- Deputy superintendent, assistant superintendent, Warren Township (IN) Schools
- Principal, assistant principal, and subject area teacher

Lynn Lehman, EdD, currently serves as the representative from Ball State University on the University Superintendent Search Team. He recently transitioned from a full-time appointment as assistant professor in the Department of Educational Leadership. His career before teaching at Ball State included:

- Superintendent, Noblesville (IN) Schools
- Deputy superintendent, assistant superintendent, Noblesville (IN) Schools
- Principal, assistant principal, and subject area teacher

www.ingramcontent.com/pod-product-compliance
Lightning Source LLC
Chambersburg PA
CBHW022014300426
44117CB00005B/177